Conversations with V. S. Naipaul

Literary Conversations Series

Peggy Whitman Prenshaw
General Editor

Conversations
with V. S. Naipaul

Edited by
Feroza Jussawalla

University Press of Mississippi
Jackson

Copyright © 1997 by the University Press of Mississippi
Manufactured in the United States of America

00 99 98 97   4 3 2 1

The paper in this book meets the guidelines for permanence and durability of the Committee on Production Guidelines for Book Longevity of the Council on Library Resources.

Library of Congress Cataloging-in-Publication Data

Conversations with V. S. Naipaul / edited by Feroza Jussawalla.
    p.   cm. — (Literary conversations series)
  Includes index.
  ISBN 0-87805-945-8 (cloth : alk. paper). — ISBN 0-87805-946-6
  (paper : alk. paper)
  1. Naipaul, V. S. (Vidiadhar Surajprasad), 1932–   —Interviews.
2. Authors, Trinidadian—20th century—Interviews.   3. East Indians—
West Indies—Interviews.   4. Developing countries—In literature.
5. West Indies—In literature.   I. Jussawalla, Feroza F., 1953–   .
II. Series.
PR9272.9.N32Z55   1997
823′.914—dc20   96-31419
                                                                   CIP

British Library Cataloging-in-Publication data available

Author's royalties to "Writers & Scholars"

Books by V. S. Naipaul

The Mystic Masseur. London: André Deutsch, 1957.
The Suffrage of Elvira. London: André Deutsch, 1958.
Miguel Street. London: André Deutsch; New York: Vanguard, 1959.
A House for Mr. Biswas. London: André Deutsch; New York: McGraw-H
   1961.
The Middle Passage. London: André Deutsch; New York: Macmillan, 196
Mr. Stone and the Knights Companion. London: André Deutsch; New Yo
   Macmillan, 1963.
An Area of Darkness. London: André Deutsch, 1964.
The Mimic Men. London: André Deutsch; New York: Macmillan, 1967.
A Flag on the Island. London: André Deutsch; New York: Macmillan, 19
The Loss of El Dorado. London: André Deutsch, 1969.
In a Free State. London: André Deutsch; New York: Knopf, 1971.
The Overcrowded Barracoon. London: André Deutsch, 1972.
Guerillas. London: André Deutsch; New York: Knopf, 1975.
India: A Wounded Civilization. London: André Deutsch; New York: Kno
A Bend in the River. London: André Deutsch; New York: Knopf, 1979.
The Return of Eva Peron, with The Killings in Trinidad. London: André
   New York: Knopf, 1980.
Among the Believers: An Islamic Journey. London: André Deutsch; Ne
   Knopf, 1981.
Finding the Center: Two Narratives. London: André Deutsch; New Yo
   Knopf, 1984.
The Enigma of Arrival. London: André Deutsch; New York: Knopf, 19
A Turn in the South. London: André Deutsch; New York: Knopf, 1989.
India: A Million Mutinies Now. London: André Deutsch; New York: V
   1990.
A Way in the World. London: Heinemann; New York: Knopf, 1994.

Contents

Introduction

Sir V. S. Naipaul's interviews are best described by the subtitle of James Atlas's interview "V. S. vs the Rest" included here and first published in *Vanity Fair*: "The Fierce and Enigmatic V. S. Naipaul Grants a Rare Interview." This collection of interviews with V. S. Naipaul, or Sir V. S. as he is sometimes called, shows the changing faces of the enigmatic Naipaul. This collection spans thirty-six years of interviews. The interviews are really not that rare; there are approximately forty-five of them, of which twenty-two are reproduced here. The early interviews are clipped, short, brusque, showing his impatience with interviewers. For instance to Fitzroy Frazer, Naipaul said in 1960, "One can't prognosticate about literature, the way one can about say, the weather." Or again in the landmark interview in this early period with Derek Walcott, Naipaul dismisses national pride in writers and cricketers with, "I am not a cricketer." This interview with the future Nobel Laureate is ironic in that Walcott was awarded the Nobel prize before the prolific V. S. Naipaul who has been on the Nobel short list for a long time now, as several of the interviews note.

The 1990s have brought a change in Naipaul. His interview with Stephen Schiff is warm, passionate, revealing—opening up areas of his private life—his relationship with his wife and the great passion of his life, an "other" love, almost as if he were priming Schiff to write the much-touted biography for which Naipaul had been searching for an author. *The Daily Telegraph* reported on this interview in "V. S. Naipaul Unveils a Past Full of Passion" (16 May 1994), noting that Naipaul rarely grants interviews and had never before discussed his infidelities. The 1990s also seem to have brought a spate of interviews, a willingness to talk that is taken up by eager young journalists. And this is the hallmark of these recent interviews; they are given to journalists and not to literary figures, while the early interviews were given to fellow writers and colleagues—Derek Walcott, the poet Eric Roach, and Ewart Rouse.

Most important though, the interviews collected in this volume show the *bildungsroman* or journey from innocence to awareness of the writer Vidiadhar Surajprasad Naipaul, who has moved increasingly towards his Indian subcontinental self as manifest in *India: A Million Mutinies Now*

(1990) and in his recent marriage to Nadira Alvi, a subcontinental woman, which affirms a return to his "Asiatic" self. The interviews trace a veritable journey from his innocence as a colonial subject from Trinidad, to a period of his "fall"—his period of distancing himself from his cultural and spiritual roots. To Adrian Rowe-Evans, he said in a *Transition* interview: "And then I belonged to a minority group, I moved away, became a foreigner, became a writer; you see the degrees of removal from direct involvement, from direct fear." But then he had also said to Derek Walcott, one cannot ever "abandon one's allegiance to one's community or at any rate to the idea of one's community." From *The Enigma of Arrival* onward there is a period of his spiritual awakening and awareness as an Indian or as he would call it "an Asiatic," a term, he tells Bharati Mukherjee in the interview published in *Salmagundi* and reprinted here, he prefers to Asian. Naipaul is (re)connecting with his roots.

In this sense the interviews collected here are almost a *roman*—a novel, a story about someone who might as well be a fictional character who is growing, developing, changing and finally coming to a knowledge of who he is. Like Rudyard Kipling's beloved character Kim, Naipaul comes to an awareness of himself, "I AM; I am Kim—the Biblical injunction 'I am that I AM.' " Just as Kipling's *Kim* remained in a B.B.C. poll even in 1996 the most read and most beloved of British books, Naipaul remains the most beloved and widely read British author. A favorite of Queen Elizabeth II, by whom he was knighted, Naipaul, as seen throughout these interviews, holds unswervingly to "I AM Naipaul," expressing his individuality, his quirkiness, and finally his spiritual awakening in Hindu Brahminhood, a feature that clearly emerges in the interviews. James Atlas, Charles Michener, Scott Winokur, and Steven Schiff all note his fanatical vegetarianism. In his interview with Charles Wheeler, he notes that Indians have lost connection with their historic past; to Bharati Mukherjee he wonders why Indians search for European ways of thinking and interpretation when they had many hundreds of years of their own; and to Andrew Robinson he says that he sees India as going through a vast regenerative period—much like what he is going through himself.

Because his own evolution is so intensely biographically connected to and mirrored in his writing, the nature of several of the interviews is largely biographical. The most poignant, poetic telling of his early life is in the interview with David Bates published in *The Sunday Times Magazine* (26 May 1963). He is in this interview a colonial subject who leaves a colonial land and is adapting to the cross-cultural situation of being in Oxford and then in London in "impenetrable seedy-poetic suburbia." In several subsequent interviews with Ian Hamilton, Charles Michener, Andrew Robinson, Stephen Schiff, and Scott Winokur, this theme returns. Andrew Robinson notes in "Going Back for a Turn in the East," "He can never forget that he is the grandson of an indentured laborer who left eastern India for Trinidad." All this flows into his "growing up," as it were, in England, learning to express his passions and connect with women, not knowing the art of seduction; suffering a breakdown for two years and forcing himself out of it through an act of will; being asthmatic and sick in a cousin's basement apartment near Paddington and rushing from one hospital to another for his asthma injections; working at the National Portrait Gallery, a cement company, and finally the B.B.C. where he eventually takes over Henry Swanzy's position as director of the "Caribbean Voices" program. Even after he married his loyal companion Pat Hale, with whom he lived for forty-one years until her death in January 1996, there were years spent in moves from many small apartments—one described particularly well by Linda Blandford. The final face of his persona and the final stage of his journey, articulated in his autobiographical *An Enigma of Arrival* (1987) and echoed in all the later interviews, is the search for his spirituality and his identity as a solitary figure making his "way in the world" and who has now come to rest in his "Asiatic" self at Salisbury near Stonehenge, the only other spiritual center of the world besides the Himalayas.

Naipaul never forgot his early beginnings and speaks out in the Ian Hamilton interview collected here for fairer treatment of the West Indian blacks. To Israel Shenker in *The New York Times Book Review* (17 October 1971, 4, 22–24), Naipaul had said that "the British have a Sunday school reaction" to slavery. They focus on the efforts to abolish it rather than on the "horrors of the crime." This is why he doesn't want exoticized or romanticized depictions of third world countries. In this, his is an early expression of the same sentiments expressed in Edward Said's *Orientalism*. To Adrian Rowe-Evans, he excoriates third world writers, both Indians and Africans, for exoticizing their countries for the benefit of their London markets—writing about what he calls "tribal" practices and localisms. "Tribal" is one of Naipaul's favorite words. He accuses everyone from Singer (in his interview with Cathleen Medwick in *Vogue* [August 1981, 129–30] when she asks him about a writer having roots) to John Cheever and even Hemingway and Elvis followers of "tribalism." In other words, he rejects, as do contemporary literary critics, exotic representations of local cultures.

Of Naipaul, Said has commented, "The most attractive and immoral

move however has been Naipaul's who has allowed himself quite consciously to be turned into a witness for the Western prosecution. There
are others like him who specialize in the thesis of what one of them has
called self-inflicted wounds, which is to say that we 'non-Whites' are the
cause of all our problems, not the overly maligned imperialists'' (*Salmagundi* Spring–Summer 1986, 53). The whole drama of a Saidian perspective versus Naipaul's is played out in two key interviews collected here,
one with Bharati Mukherjee and Robert Boyers and another with Scott
Winokur. C. L. R. James, the Trinidadian Socialist activist, is central to
this discussion. Schiff posits that Lebrun, a character in *A Way in the
World*, is "transparently" based on C. L. R. James. In his 1968 interview
with Ewart Rouse, Naipaul expressed great respect for James's *Beyond a
Boundary*, and to Andrew Robinson in 1992 he still expressed this
admiration. *A Bend in the River* raises readers' consciousnesses against
pirated African art in modernist galleries and against the Afrophile who
loots primitive art for U.S. galleries. Naipaul speaks repeatedly about the
obligations of the writer to tell the truth as he sees it. Aamer Hussein's
interview nicely encapsulates this. As Robert Boyers says in Scott
Winokur's interview, "There's something grotesque about demanding of
a world-class writer that he hew to a partyline or an ethnic perspective.''
  Naipaul is quite outspoken about developing one's own forms of
culturally contextualized literary criticism. He notes to Adrian Rowe-
Evans about Chinua Achebe: "His work needs the blessing of the foreign
market . . . because the local doesn't have any body of judgements as it
can't trust itself to make its own appraisals.'' Naipaul describes to
Charles Wheeler Indian analysts "mimicking other people's intellectual
disciplines.'' He pursues this line of thinking with Bharati Mukherjee.
When the behavior of the people and the degeneration of the land is what
he can't abide, Naipaul will speak plainly about it whether it offends
people or not. He can turn his wrath equally on the benevolent paternal-
ism of "white pseudo-intellectuals,'' as Scott Winokur has called them.
  Naipaul also would not want to be called a postcolonial. He calls these
categories slightly "bogus'' (another of his favorite words). James Atlas
notes that Naipaul dropped a publisher who made the mistake of advertising him as a "West Indian writer.'' It was too political a term. Naipaul
has seen himself repeatedly as a colonial writing with the "ridiculous
panic'' of a colonial, but he has distanced himself from the politics and
prejudices of postcoloniality.
  Naipaul tells us throughout these interviews that attaching oneself to
other cultures is to be superficial. To Cathleen Medwick he says his work
is about people who want "to attach themselves . . . to other civilizations,

with other drives," because "their own have failed them. But these people only succeed in becoming aliens with no sense of who they are, or why they have come." In this Naipaul is very much like Kipling, who denounces in *Kim* "the monstrous hybridism of East and West." And Naipaul is not a "bogus" holy man peddling false spirituality like his G. Ramsay Muir, or like the India he criticizes for not having anything to show after all these years of wisdom but false holy men. He doesn't care if you're not on "the journey(s)" with him. He lives his own search, finding the center.

Naipaul has come the full Karmic circle in knowing where he belongs. Alex Hamilton noted in his interview with Naipaul after he had chosen Naipaul for the Booker prize that he has become "paradoxically a wheel, the weight of his obsessions at a tangent to any society in which he finds himself." ("Living a Life on Approval," *Manchester Guardian* 4 October 1971, 8). He has made his journey from the initial culture contact, the absorption into the colonizers' frame of mind, a move towards hybridity, and a final coming to one's recognition of himself as belonging to the culture that he started from. This is a typical "postcolonial *bildungs-roman.*"

From the late 1970s on, Naipaul focuses on a search for form rather than style, the importance of which he dismisses to Bharati Mukherjee in 1981. Until then, he had "played elegantly with the inelegancies of West Indian English." His entire career though has been a search for an appropriate postcolonial style and form which he has crystallized in *A Way in the World.* In the earliest available interview conducted by Fitzroy Frazer in 1960, Naipaul calls his novels "an accident"—a form that came to him as he worked. In the most recent interviews, one with the renowned Commonwealth Literature scholar Alastair Niven and with the *Far Eastern Economic Review*'s Ahmed Rashid (an interview reprinted in *The Guardian* on February 25, 1996), he justifies his new form. To Alastair Niven, he provides a fuller justification, a note on his growth into his new form: "The novel ambition was given to me by my father. He had derived it from his reading and to me that was where the nobility in writing lay. When I developed problems with moving on, having exhausted the early impulses, I discovered that there was a whole world to write about in other ways." Like the authors James Joyce and Salman Rushdie and even the Indian writer Raja Rao who found the novel form so inadequate for expressing their local sensibilities, Naipaul found it wanting and moved on to a mixture of history, travel writing, and fiction. Naipaul was seeking independence from the foreign form imposed on

non-English writers. The last interviews with Aamer Hussein, Ahmed
Rashid and Alastair Niven speak eloquently to this issue.

In his interviews, Naipaul refutes the charges of selling out his cultures
and of being colonialist and creating colonialist discourse. He is merely
"seeing ourselves as others see us" and in so doing seeing into the heart
of things. Though Naipaul would object strongly to being categorized as
a postcolonial, these interviews embody his attitude of postcoloniality.
They show the "twenty layers of self" that we all have, of which Naipaul
talked in our brief conversation at the University of Tulsa's After Empire
Conference in March 1994.

There are many themes in the Naipaul interviews that repeat themselves. Charles Michener notes that his friends say Naipaul talks in *bis*,
i.e., in repetitions. This is true. To Frank Winstone he had said, "Not
even a million dollars could gag him" (*Sunday Mirror* [Trinidad] 26 April
1964). To Adrian Rowe-Evans and to Israel Shenker, he repeats this line,
then says he's changed his mind. He'd gone on too long. To Elizabeth
Hardwick and to Bharati Mukherjee he says "Indians have had too many
people loving them for their wretchedness." The most insistent theme
without variation is that of "panic," which Keith Hamish called "the
ridiculous panic behind Vidia Naipaul" (*Trinidad Guardian* 29 November
1972, p. 9). To Naipaul this panic is not ridiculous. He feels it over and
over again and talks about it over and over again—the panic of the writer,
the panic of survival, the panic that pulls him through his career. Another
theme is the short listing for the Nobel Prize and the subsequent disappointments.

In interviewing Naipaul, Stephen Schiff talks about hearing the dithyramb of "No I don't want to talk about this." James Atlas and Scott
Winokur talk about how difficult it is to interview Naipaul. Captain
Moonlight in his "notebook" in *The Independent on Sunday* (18 April
1993) reports that Ian Buruma, who has been chosen as Naipaul's
biographer, is reported to have bouts of terror in Naipaul's presence.
Interviewers everywhere have noted as Stephen Schiff does that Naipaul
wants the questions rephrased. If they're offensive, he simply leaves as
he left the Dutch lights, camera, and action on a book tour. "Instead of
coming to me and asking 'Why did you write this book?' you should be
saying 'How did you see so much?' " Schiff quotes him as saying.
Another theme that repeats itself is Naipaul's disdain for academics.
Andrew Robinson in his interview, "Stranger in Fiction," notes the
exasperation with "the pretend Marxists in Western universities" where
Marxism is used as a "posture." Naipaul has been critical of academia

per se whether it was teaching at the University in Kampala, Uganda (1966), or at Wesleyan.

He has also described his method of composing over the years. To Derek Walcott he says that he writes down impressions, maybe a word or so and then composes around these. In other interviews, particularly to Scott Winokur, he says that his method of creating *India: A Million Mutinies Now* was largely to carry a small copy book in his blue silk jacket pocket and to jot down notes after a conversation or to take dictation.

Some interviews contain the seeds of works to come. For instance, in one interview not included here but excerpted in *The Listener* from a 1973 radio program (22 March 1973, 367–68, 370), Naipaul seems to have started *A Way in the World* in his own mind. To Ronald Bryden, Naipaul talks about Las Casas:

> And there's that marvelous story which is told about the Inca, Garcilaso de la Vega. Garcilaso was the son of a Peruvian princess and a Spanish Conquistador. He decided when he was quite a young man that history was flowing in the direction of Europe and Spain, so he went to Spain. One day, when he was very old, Bartolome de Las Casas, the apostle of the Indians, a great friend of the Indians, saw a man across a room who was clearly an Indian from the New World and went across to him and said very friendlily, "You're from Mexico, aren't you?" Garcilaso, recognising Las Casas, said, "No, I'm from Peru," and both men at once knew that in a most ridiculous and grotesque way they were on opposite sides.

Thus the interviews contain information germane to understanding the development of Naipaul's work.

What I hope I have shown through this collection is that V. S. Naipaul is not the man made out by his critics—a standoffish critic of the third world seeing all postcolonial countries as "areas of darkness." The interviews show a man struggling with his own identity as well as his loyalty to his Indian family—at once a fierce, independent man struggling to break free of family, community, and identity and a little boy in need of solace, a desire to talk out and write out his psychological problems of family Indian and British, of nation and of the lack of belonging—a pull between home versus hybridity. And this is the enigma of "the fierce Naipaul," who like the Brahmin in the last chapter of *The Enigma of Arrival* (347), "Ceremony of Farewell," offers himself like a sacrifice with the words "swa-ha": "Om Bhur Buh swa ha" ["the One Power and

One Presence, God the good, omnipotent"]. This is a move towards "Shruddha"—spiritual oneness, merging with the fire.

As with other books in the Literary Conversations Series, the interviews are reprinted uncut. In newspaper interviews, paragraph breaks have been omitted; titles of books have been italicized; and typographical errors have been silently corrected. Inevitably, there is a certain amount of repetition in the interviews as Naipaul was asked the same questions and he inevitably gave the same answers. On some issues, he remains consistent, and on some, as I have pointed out, he changes his mind. No two interviews are exactly alike. Each adds to the portrait of this remarkable individual.

I would like to thank all those who helped track down interviews and authors that were extremely difficult to find: the Newspaper Library at Colindale; the *Trinidad Guardian* and the National Heritage Library; Claire Maidana and Simon Read at the B.B.C.; Diana Pepper at the *Independent* and the authors who generously gave of their material, particularly Aamer Hussein for providing me a copy of his interview together with his permission; Ahmed Rashid for readily giving permission; Andrew Robinson for generously providing permission to use all his work; Nobel Laureate Derek Walcott; Jim Douglas Henry, who also helped me find other *Listener* authors; Elizabeth Hardwick, particularly for her graciousness; Peggy Boyers; Mel Gussow; Pamela Scott of *The San Francisco Examiner*; Wylovyn Gager at *The Jamaica Gleaner*; Carl Jacobs of the *Trinidad Guardian*; and Sid Huttner at the University of Tulsa.

On the home front my efforts in this book are dedicated to my mother who is an inveterate clipper-outer of newspapers wherever she is around the world and without whose assistance I would not have been able to collect many of the current overseas interviews; to my mother-in-law Mary Esther Dasenbrock for financial assistance with the phone, fax, and copier bills; to my husband Reed and my son Homi for loving support, patience, and assistance; to the interlibrary loan librarians at UTEP, Carolyn Kahl, Olga Nervaez, and Debbie Morgan; to Rosa Holguin-Hernandez for her help with permissions; to graduate dean Julie Sanford and the then dean of my college Carl Jackson, for their financial support. Finally, I must thank Bonnie E. Elder for her expert typing and for making sense of an extremely hard-to-read manuscript. My editor Seetha Srinivasan waited patiently for the book to be put together and pushed hard for its completion. I am grateful for her.

Finally I would like to thank anyone who has helped with this book in any way, answering questions, providing materials and information and assistance in general. Most important, I would like to thank V. S. Naipaul for being a most interesting subject to work on. These sparkling interviews serve as inspiration for aspiring writers. It is for their immense educational value to writers, students, scholars and for the archival purpose of bringing together hard to find interviews from now defunct journals and newspapers that these interviews have been gathered here. For this I am sure generations of students will thank Mr. Naipaul and his interviewers. From V. S. Naipaul, I have learned much about "seeing ourselves as others see us" and speaking and living our truth as we see it.

---

*Intext citations are given for interviews not included in this book.

Chronology

1932   Born August 17, in Chagunas, Trinidad; second of seven chil-
        dren—Naipaul had one brother and five sisters; son of Seeper-
        sad Naipaul, journalist, grandson of a Hindu indentured la-
        borer, a Brahmin.

1933   Father threatened with death for article on farmers doing
        Kali puja

1950   Arrives in England to go to Oxford

1951   Suffers depression at Oxford

1953   Father dies; Naipaul gets his degree in English from University
        College, Oxford.

1954   Moves to London with six pounds; works at a cement company
        for ten months; works at B.B.C. as editor of "Caribbean
        Voices."

1955   Marries Patricia Hale

1957   Moves to Kilburn, Streatham Hill; *The Mystic Masseur*, Lon-
        don, André Deutsch, and in 1959 published by Vanguard Press,
        New York; Llewellyn Rhys Memorial Prize.

1958   *The Suffrage of Elvira*, London, André Deutsch

1959   *Miguel Street*, London, André Deutsch and New York, Van-
        guard; Somerset Maugham Award

1960   Commissioned by the Premier of Trinidad, Eric Williams, to
        write a book of nonfiction about the West Indies; seven months
        in West Indies and South America; "The Middle Passage"
        written.

1961   *A House for Mr. Biswas*, London, André Deutsch and New
        York, McGraw-Hill

1962   Travel to India; *Mr. Stone and the Knights Companion* written;

The Middle Passage, London, André Deutsch and New York, Macmillan.

1963   *Mr. Stone and the Knights Companion*, London, André Deutsch and New York, Macmillan; Hawthornden Prize.

1964   *An Area of Darkness*, London, André Deutsch and in 1965 published by Macmillan, New York

1966   At University of Kampala, Uganda

1967   *The Mimic Men*, London, André Deutsch and New York, Macmillan; W.H. Smith Prize; *A Flag on the Island*, London, André Deutsch and New York, Macmillan.

1969   *The Loss of El Dorado*, London, André Deutsch and in 1970 published by Knopf, New York

1971   *In a Free State*, London, André Deutsch and New York, Knopf; Booker Prize; moves to cottage in Wiltshire.

1972   Lecture tour of New Zealand for International Book Year; *The Overcrowded Barracoon*, London, André Deutsch and in 1973 published by Knopf, New York.

1975   *Guerillas*, London, André Deutsch and New York, Knopf

1977   *India: A Wounded Civilization*, London, André Deutsch and New York, Knopf

1978   Distinguished Writer in Residence, Wesleyan University, Middletown, CT

1979   *A Bend in the River*, London, André Deutsch and New York, Knopf

1980   *The Return of Eva Peron, with The Killings in Trinidad*, London, André Deutsch and New York, Knopf

1981   *Among the Believers: An Islamic Journey*, London, André Deutsch and New York, Knopf

1984   *Finding the Center: Two Narratives*, London, André Deutsch and New York, Knopf; attends Republican Convention in Dallas, Texas.

1987   *The Enigma of Arrival*, London, André Deutsch and New York, Knopf

1989   *A Turn in the South*, London, André Deutsch and New York,
        Knopf

1990   *India: A Million Mutinies Now*, London, André Deutsch and
        New York, Viking; Knighthood, Queen's New Year List.

1993   First winner of David Cohen British Literature Prize

1994   *A Way in the World*, London, Heinemann and New York,
        Knopf

1996   January: Patricia Hale dies; 18 April: marries Nadira Alvi.

Conversations with V. S. Naipaul

A Talk with Vidia Naipaul

Fitzroy Fraser / 1960

From *The Sunday Gleaner* (Jamaica), 25 December 1960, 14, 10. Reprinted by permission of The Gleaner Company Limited.

Scarborough, Tobago: He came in the afternoon, complete with liveried chauffeur and the administration car—signs of the $600 that's his for another month or so. For he's back in Trinidad & Tobago now on the first of three months' fellowships given—it took him by surprise—by the Government of Trinidad & Tobago to their artists working abroad.

His clothes looked informal and comfortable. A soft, open-necked shirt, a pair of khaki slacks, newish brown sandals. No socks. Tie was short, and his softish voice spoke in bursts, somewhat like a Bren Gun probing gently into No Man's Land. His thick black hair hung almost down to his ear. In a way, he looked like Kingsley Amis. The main difference was the colour of his skin.

Just then he seemed perturbed at the way Tobagonians carry on their affairs—the slow reticent, informal, unsure hesitancy and vacillation of the Lords of Scarborough.

But later—in the evening, he seemed to have recovered the poise to reach his English accent. He seemed to have lost the venom which he had when last here two years ago, which made him label the society which spurned him (and perhaps truly) as "Philistine." Just now, this society, one "vertical and complex" seemed just a mass of easy morass.

Just now, his complaint was that he still couldn't work here—or in Trinidad: for in neither place was there the isolation on which he thrives and which, while at work, he lives in for days. So much so that it makes "going out to buy a loaf of bread an adventure."

The rooms in the houses here still had 50 watt bulbs in the ceiling, and were too open. No, it was quite impossible.

Furthermore he couldn't remain here for long without getting stung by the money-bug. He couldn't be poor here and feel comfortable. Poverty it seemed, was something like a crime.

All through the evening, his tone was that of one studiously unwilling to offend. If he had to make a point, it was done usually with a rhetorical question and a throaty laugh that suggested a cold in his stomach.

He lit a cigarette, and toyed with it for a while, then he turned his chair

3

away from the table, rested an arm across the back of the chair, and started playing with the silver-coloured lighter, twirling it around in his hand like a tiny yo-yo.

He had on a dark suit, now, and a reddish looking tie, and the tone and stress in his voice, especially when he mentioned the word "society," made you think of home and maybe the way Morris Cargill mouths the same word.

No, he didn't think that creative writers should get involved in such things as the wind of Nationalism which is now gathering force down here in the Southern Caribbean. West Indian novels so far had too much sex, some of it larded and pasted in; so he couldn't see them being used in West Indian schools. Still there could of course be expurgated editions, the way some editors did Shakespeare. But then he wasn't quite sure that anything even closely resembling a book would be left. All that might be left would be a pamphlet. So, there.

George Lamming, he thought "very brilliant," while Edgar Mittleholzer was "very versatile." How else could Mittleholzer manage to do two novels a year? "He just finishes one, then puts a new sheet of paper in the typewriter and writes, Chapter One."

Naipaul himself, doesn't quite work in that way. He goes along and works as work comes to him. In a way, his novels have been "an accident." The fourth, which his publishers are putting out next year, took him more than a year to write. And as to the actual substance of his work, as to the stylized Trinidadian dialect he uses, it's so because that's the true speech of the characters he deals with—Ramlogan (*The Suffrage of Elvira*), Ganesh Ramsumair (*The Mystic Masseur*), or even Bogart (*Miguel Street*).

West Indian novels, he said hadn't made a big impact on the English reading public. And even the critics who had been so enthusiastic about them were beginning to react against them. As to poetry, it was much worse. It couldn't hope to be much more than a "labour of love." He was non-committal about the drama, but he did, in passing mention the colossal failure that was Barry Beckford's *Flesh to a Tiger*.

As to the future, he wouldn't commit himself. One can't prognosticate about literature, the way one can about say, the weather.

It was there—if it came—and should be used. That was all.

At the same time, he refused to be drawn into saying who he thought was the best novelist the Southern Caribbean has so far produced.

It was time to get to Della Mina's for a bash.

Interview with V. S. Naipaul

Derek Walcott / 1965

From *Sunday Guardian* (Trinidad), 7 March 1965, 5, 7. Reprinted by permission of Derek Walcott.

V. S. Naipaul, the celebrated novelist, returned to his native Trinidad recently for a short visit. Mr. Naipaul, who has been acclaimed by critics as one of the most accomplished young writers, lives in England.

His last book, *An Area of Darkness*, describes a year's stay in India. It has aroused as much controversy as his other work of non-fiction, *The Middle Passage*, which dealt with the West Indies.

Mr. Naipaul has been the recipient of several awards for literature. He is the author of *Miguel Street*, *The Mystic Masseur*, *The Suffrage of Elvira*, *Mr. Stone and the Knights Companion* and *A House for Mr. Biswas*, which is considered his masterpiece.

Derek Walcott: The last time you were here you were working on *The Middle Passage* . . .

Mr. Naipaul: Yes. The Government has granted me this scholarship to return and suggested that I might write a book . . . which, after some hesitation, I decided to do. I hesitated largely because it was non-fiction and at that time I felt I could not write non-fiction because it was not my thing.

I still find non-fiction extremely difficult; that is having to reduce disordered ideas into order. The most difficult book I have written is this book on India. I finished it a year ago and I am still exhausted.

The thing about travelling is that it is always slightly repetitive; the events of one day seem to occur on the next and so on. After a few months in India, it seemed that I had nothing to write about. In fact, while I was there I abandoned the idea of writing a book. But I had already taken some money from my publishers and if I didn't present them with a book of sorts I would have had to refund the money.

What is your method of compiling? Did you use a diary in India?

I used a diary for *The Middle Passage* but for the Indian book I used no diary at all. It was about ten to twelve weeks after I got back that I began to try to write something. And then it was like playing with the beginning of a novel, you know; looking for the pattern in confused

impressions. Writing a word like "ruins" on a copybook page and looking
at it for a day.

*Your book about India seems to me much more profound: there is a
greater feeling of reaction. Is this the result of looking more deeply into
the Indian society?*
This difference is the difference in societies. Trinidad is a haphazard
sort of society, India appears to be more profound, but the principle of
Indian society is a simple one. Because this society is self-contained and
unique, it is possible to get at the truth, or to appear to get at it,
more easily.

*In your book you mentioned you felt a certain anonymity in going back
to India. Now you are back in your native country, do you feel you can
resume your identification with Indians here or do you feel completely
isolated in this society?*
I do not think one can ever abandon one's allegiance to one's community, or at any rate to the idea of one's community. This is something I
feel must be said.

*I don't mean that one can detach oneself from one's community. I
mean do you feel in any sense displaced in either country; displaced on
your return here?*
Oh, yes. I find this place frightening. I think this is a very sinister place.

What particular elements in this society make it sinister?
So many middle-class people I meet here are insecure and unfulfilled.
They act and react on one another all the time to produce this odd
communal destructive instinct. Also, manners here are not very good.

*Would you extend that to include the behaviour of the entire society?
Do you mean the mores or the behaviour of the society as a whole or do
you mean that most people don't have any manners?*
I mean it in both senses. In the old colonial society there was an
element of aspiration. This was the motive of the society. You know, one
felt so far away from the centre of the world. Like the Muslims in
Cordoba always trying to catch up with the boys in Beirut. We aimed
high and we produced a lot of bright people.
Possibly, these impressions are superficial—goodness, I am now in the
middle of this Carnival thing which I dislike very much—but I feel, you
know, that aspiration has been dropped, that the manners of the proletariat have infiltrated the values of the rest of society.
I notice this also, in the old days young people at school made an effort

to speak well. Today this has been abandoned. Go to the law courts.
Some witnesses still try. The lawyers don't. Possibly, this is the mark of
a good lawyer . . . .

*Are you saying standards have been lowered to meet the rising de-
mands of the proletariat?*
Yes, the threat of the proletariat. But I mean more than standards. I
feel the culture has changed. I think this is true not only of Trinidad: it is
true of England as well. Political views are now being imposed on the top
from below. And fashions. And entertainments.

Where do you locate yourself in all this?
I see all these things as very hostile to me and the things I try to do. I
am very distressed by them. Especially in a place like England where it
is now being glamorised. You've got this word "pop." Pop art, pop this
and pop that. A pacifying euphemism. So now they've got pop politics
as well.

*In the West Indies, particularly in Trinidad, reaction of the society to
your achievements has been one of pride. This, of course, might not be
of particular interest to you. I think Lamming mentioned something
about this in his book; the connection between writers and even cricketers
and their society. How do you feel about this?*
I am not a cricketer.

But this connection is inevitable, is it not?
To the writer it is incidental. So it should be, don't you think? But I
also believe the fact that people who write about a society ennoble that
society. The fact that the society produces writers is a credit to the
society. I have grown out of Trinidad and in a way I am grateful to the
Trinidad I knew as a boy for making me what I am. I do not carry
tremendous chips on my shoulder.

*Do you think that having lived in Trinidad, in a multi-racial society,
has helped you to achieve a more balanced perception? For example, a
writer brought up in Trinidad does not have the same racial belligerence
as a Jamaican writer. The two societies are different. In your work there
is a very delicate sense of humour. One finds this in Selvon also. Do you
see your ability to laugh at certain situations, not with mockery necessarily, as part of having been brought up in Trinidad?*
I really don't know . . . .

*Characters in Miguel Street, for example, I think you have drawn them
with a great deal of tenderness and compassion . . . .*

I wouldn't like to have them to breakfast. Writing, I think, is a very fraudulent thing. When you start writing about something it changes. It becomes distorted. It is extremely hard for a writer to know what is going to happen when he starts writing about a particular thing.

A well-known English novelist went to Kenya during the Mau-Mau emergency. His sympathies were with the Kikuyu; and it was for this reason that he couldn't write a novel about the emergency. He didn't know what would have come out. What I am trying to say is this: in the process of writing one might discover deeper truths about oneself which might be slightly different from the day to day truth about one's reaction.

Some of your critics claim that you laugh at people. This, for instance, was one of the immediate criticisms of The Middle Passage. *How do you feel about this?*

I have never been aware that I am laughing at people. It would be bad manners and pointless writing. I think this is the reaction of insecurity, though. In a few years people won't always require the figure of the sad black struggler.

In a previous conversation you said you prefer to be described as an ironist rather than a satirist. Why?

I am not a satirist. Satire comes out of a tremendous impulse of optimism. One simply does not indulge in satire when one is awaiting death. Satire is a type of anger. Irony and comedy, I think, come out of a sense of acceptance.

Are you active in politics?

No, to be active in politics is, in a way, to over estimate the capacity of the animal.

Would you commit yourself to a side in any clearly defined cause?

You cannot commit yourself unless your cause is absolutely pure. I think there have really been only two good causes within recent times: against Hitler and possibly in South Africa which represents the absolute triumph of a European proletarian culture. Places like Australia, New Zealand really proletarian extensions and South Africa, these are of England.

In Rhodesia, you know, when the newsreels show train accidents in which Africans are killed the English applaud. This is how a civilisation dies. Look at what has been happening in England, in Smethwick. Griffiths and his followers represent, in a way, the most important thinking in the Conservative Party which they hope would win them the next elections.

Do you want to talk about style? This should be interesting because I know how difficult prose is, particularly clear prose. And what I admire about your style is its precision and lucidity.

I do not believe in natural genius. I do not believe in the spontaneous outpouring of soul. Style is essentially a matter of hard thinking; it is knowing exactly what you want and to say—that is the hard part—and then you've got this wonderful thing called language which you use.

Do you write in paragraphs?

No. I always write solidly, in sections, then break them up into paragraphs. I find it very hard to write in deliberate paragraphs.

I have observed your prose becoming more structured, your sentences becoming more syntactically involved . . .

Yes, I am aware of this. I think this represents the way one thinks. Probably, this results from solitude. If you remain by yourself for some time you will find this happening. When you go out and begin speaking to people you will find yourself using more complicated and formal language. It is also becoming harder to make simple, straight forward statements. One always wants to go back, to correct, to qualify. One is saying more difficult things as well. In this Indian book, for example, one has said so many difficult things.

What has been the reaction from India?

I think very good. Non-Indians have been more disturbed. The quality newspapers in India and the intellectuals have been very good. They too are sick of the Indian spirituality and ancient culture business. Others believe the book is all about defecation. I begin to feel that I coined the word and devised the act. But there are only six pages in which the subject has been analysed.

What were the hard years?

The very hard years were . . . goodness, I don't think they are over. One is still very anxious. I think it was in '58 that I ceased to be destitute, really. Up to that time I was almost pennyless. Yet this did not matter to one. I remember I had just one tie and when I bought a new one I used to drop the old one into the waste paper basket in the shop.

Did you ever think of abandoning writing?

I actually did in '57. I abandoned writing and took a job as an advertising copy writer which I held for ten weeks.

Do you meet any English writers?

Yes, but they are fairly old people, nearing their sixties. I see very few of . . . get along better with older people. *me too*

Naipaul: An Interview with Ewart Rouse

Ewart Rouse / 1968

From *Trinidad Guardian*, Thursday, 28 November 1968, 9, 13.
Reprinted by permission of *Trinidad Guardian*.

peccat

Vidia Naipaul, the celebrated Trinidad-born novelist, does not consider himself a West Indian novelist. And it is hardly likely that he will write anything more about the West Indies or West Indian situations.

"I feel I no longer know the place," he said yesterday, in an interview at a private home at Valsayn Park, where he is staying during a short Trinidad holiday.

"I feel the place has changed considerably. I don't think the change is in myself."

Naipaul explained that his writing has long ceased to be West Indian; that *Mimic Men*, his latest novel, was more about London than anything else.

"In fact, this is why it has been well received in England," he said. "Many people thought that someone had written about London in an interesting way."

Naipaul rejected any idea of his being West Indian, or a West Indian writer. "I don't know what the word means," he said.

"I have nothing in common with the people from Jamaica," he added. "Or the other islands for that matter. I don't understand them. As a writer I have to make a living and I certainly don't believe I can make a living by being regional.

"I hope my work is not regional. One likes to think that what one says would be of interest to the people who read books in various languages."

Naipaul pointed out that at present he enjoyed a London reputation, "and I think that if one has got no reputation in the United States, for example, it is because the moment people hear of the Caribbean—as one publisher told me—they think of 'those crazy resort places.'

"This," he said, "is very damaging to a writer. If a writer has to make a living in the outside world—which is concerned with the whole world and not just one area of it—to be purely regional is in fact to sink."

About West Indians in London, does he not consider them as future source material?

"Oddly enough," Naipaul replied, "they only interest me politically, not as source material."

Does he keep up with the works of West Indian novelists?

"I used to read a lot of West Indian novels until 1956. Since then I have stopped really. This is because they have stopped feeding me. It is really hard to read books that don't feed me.

"I did a review of C. L. R. James' book *Beyond a Boundary* a few years ago. I liked that very much."

Did he maintain contact with West Indian writers in London?

"The contact is more intermittent. Some I have not seen for years. We don't have anything in common, you see."

Naipaul, who arrived in Trinidad a little over a week ago and who is expected to be in Trinidad for "a few more days," indicated that it was hardly likely that he would return to Trinidad eventually to reside permanently ("you mean forever and forever?").

"I think the taxation here is sufficient deterrent to that," he said. "I think it is punitive. I think it would make me feel that I was earning money I had stolen. As one who had lived many years in poverty I would be very unhappy."

From Trinidad Naipaul pushes on to the United States where he will write a series of long articles for the *Daily Telegraph*.

"It is a pretty open assignment," he explained. "And it is part of my work."

After the U.S., he proposes to "drift" around the world. "I have no fixed base at the moment. I suppose I will drift around until I am tired, and as long as the money lasts.

"I don't want to take any fellowships. I am very frightened at becoming a parasite really. I have earned all the money I have had. I would be very frightened at getting a regular salary, whether I did anything or not for it."

He said that in the end he would probably return to London, but this may only be for "business reasons."

At present he was not doing "anything." Naipaul explained, "I do nothing between writings. I work very hard on a book, then I do nothing at all. I am usually too exhausted for anything."

He pointed out that whenever he got down to writing anything, it becomes such an obsession with him, that he seldom replies to letters.

During the rest of his "idle" period in Trinidad, Naipaul does not propose to accept any invitations to lecture, or become involved in any cultural activities. On the whole, he never accepts assignments to lecture.

"It is foolish to think that I would write 7,000 words for love. The annoying thing about being a writer is that some people think that one is willing to lend one's time and one's energy to their own endeavours."

How did he go about writing a book? "That is hard to say. I can't see how anyone can describe how a book is written. It is something which interests all serious writers. In the end, after all the descriptions, there remains a complex mystery about the course of a very serious work."

From what source would he draw for his future novels? "One tries really to write about what one knows. I think I'll write much more about England. I have spent nearly 20 years there.

"I have got to spend several months 'playing' before a book emerges. Then when I discover I have a book, I am so concerned with completing it that I have the dream that I'm going to finish it right away. The last book I was doing I thought I would finish quickly. This turned out to be 14 months."

Did he have any advice for local writers about going abroad? "I think these things are really personal. No one should really recommend anything to anyone else. One always talks from one's experience.

"Serious writers in the end always do what they feel they must. The classic rule is that no one should say 'I am going to write.' He should first get a job. I did not do that, and this was not possible for me in Trinidad."

About his own development, from his two early novels *Miguel Street* and *Suffrage of Elvira*, to *House for Mr. Biswas*, and *Mimic Men*, Naipaul said:

"I have developed very slowly. I was not a prodigy. I never wrote well at school, and I did not get top marks in composition and things like that.

"Learning to write for me was an extremely slow business. One develops through what one has written. I would hate to think one has not changed in the last 14 years, or has not developed, or tried to extend oneself. I don't think any writer wants to repeat himself. The pen will drop from his hands."

Naipaul pointed out that he worked through an agent—that he thought this desirable for any writer. "No writer can manage all his affairs. After a time being a writer is like running a small business. One must keep in touch with what is happening but one should not go rushing around doing deals for himself, for he won't have time for anything else."

He explained that he had always lived by writing, but it was only in the last three years or so that he felt he could live exclusively from his books.

"About 10 years ago, I earned no more than £15 (TT $72) a week," he said. "Two years after I had written three books, and I had £300 (TT $1,440).

"It is a very slow process making money from writing. I do not recommend it for people who want to make money right away. I was never really concerned about money. I would be quite happy if I could just keep afloat. I think that would be fine.

"It is very silly but the moment you start accruing some sort of money you got to pay it out in income tax. This drives you back. Every year you slide down the hill.

"I think the writer should be free after 15 years to rest for a while. English taxation does not afford one the opportunity to rest for a while."

Willis Barnstone

Without a Place: V. S. Naipaul in Conversation with Ian Hamilton

Ian Hamilton / 1971

From *Times Literary Supplement* 30 July 1971, 897. Reprinted by permission of Ian Hamilton.

Hamilton: *About thirteen years ago you wrote a rather gloomy article in the TLS about the problems of the regional writer. You ended the article by saying that your sense of alienation from England, from things English, had deepened to the point where you felt you had achieved the "Buddhist ideal of non-attachment". You didn't vote, you said, you didn't march or sign petitions. More importantly, though, you could not envisage much development for yourself as a writer because development would necessarily involve becoming more English than you could imagine yourself ever becoming. Since that time, however, you have moved on to tackle English subjects. English settings, and you have tackled them, it seems to me, with precisely the assurance, the intimacy, which you felt you'd always lack. Have you in fact come to feel more at home here?*

Naipaul: I think what happened is that I've begun to understand the world a lot better than I did when I wrote that piece. When I came to England in 1950 I was a thorough colonial. Now, to be a colonial is, in a way, to know a total kind of security. It is to have all decisions about major issues taken out of one's hands. It is to feel that one's political status has been settled so finally that there is very little one can do in the world. I think this is the background to a lot of my thinking at that time. I was eighteen when I came here and in a way I have grown up here. I've had a second childhood, a second becoming aware of the world. I've grown out of one attitude and begun to understand the world from another point of view, in my maturity. How much of this is England and how much is just age and how much is the act of writing I don't know. But I remain quite astonished at my political indifference. Things like Mau Mau in Kenya in 1952 passed over me completely. Suez: these things always came to me a few years late. Vietnam: at the beginning, people asked me to sign a petition in 1965. I didn't know what they were talking about, I really didn't know. This is, I think, the complete colonial attitude.

It's unlikely, though, that an eighteen-year-old immigrant today would have this attitude.

What I find very interesting is that one has ceased to be a colonial. One no longer enjoys this great security. In fact, when something like Bengal comes along, I am aware of a new difference between me and people in England. I am aware that I am the insecure person that people here are the totally secure. The cartoonists here have taken up the Oxfam Rich West-Poor East attitude. They've missed the point, which to me is that the people in Bengal are being killed by Chinese and American weapons.

I wonder, though, if your sense of "non-attachment" was peculiar, in the sense that you were an Indian who had been brought up in the West Indies, that even before you came to England you already felt remote from the political life of the country you were living in.

I don't think so. I think any remoteness there was because one saw the silliness of political life there. One saw the absurdity. People were talking about Athens. People saw that primitive society as Athens, and you couldn't buy this. One's rejection of political activity was perhaps a rejection of a very stupid kind of local colonial politician. A mistake. One should have seen that all these half-dead little territories had the possibilities of terror. The difference for me now is that while I have become less of a colonial and more aware of my own insecurity, begun to see more and more, in fact, how much one's concerns in the world are founded on one's political assumptions about the world, I think the people in England have become more colonial themselves. They have begun to feel this total security because they are attached to America. They have begun not to be interested, not to feel involved or threatened in any way. Let me put it this way. I am aware that people here think it awfully chic to take an interest in American Black Power. Now to me the American Black Power movement is a bogus sort of television revolution. I don't see what it has to do with people over here. If you are interested in Blacks, in England, then you do have Blacks to hand. Blacks whose situation is infinitely worse than that of the American Blacks. I mean the West Indian Blacks, who are people without any representation in the world whatsoever. Now here is a cause. But this cause has not been sanctified by America, it has not been sanctified by the media, it has not been sanctified by chicness.

You don't feel it has been sanctified even slightly, by Enoch Powell?

Well, exactly. But Ronald Reagan's more glamorous, and American. Though you'd have thought that with Enoch Powell there would have been here a greater concern for West Indian Blacks, for Blacks who are in Guyana, or Antigua, or Grenada, people who in the end are without representation—they have no representation here and, for all sorts of reasons, they have no representation in their own countries. They are a lost people, and I don't think anyone is interested.

To go back to the TLS article I mentioned; in it you talked not just about your alienation as an individual in a strange society but also about your relation, as a writer, to the literature of England. You have been brought up on that literature and you were writing in English, but you could see no way of connecting your own work to the English literary tradition.

This remains totally true. I am aware that it is very nearly impossible for me to have the great pleasure of a direct response from an audience. And perhaps because I don't have this I think of it as a great pleasure. By the nature of one's situation one is really writing in a vacuum. I couldn't have become a writer without London—the whole physical apparatus of publishing, of magazines, the BBC. This apparatus enables a man to make a living. London is my metropolitan centre, it is my commercial centre, and yet I know that it is a kind of limbo and that I am a refugee in the sense that I am always peripheral. One's concerns are not the concerns of local people.

You don't think you are being too gloomy, too self-deprecating even about your lostness as a writer? You might feel that you can never be an English writer and yet the techniques, the strategies, much of the style of even your earliest books are such as can be instantly recognized and relished by an English reader and with the added pleasure of seeing them focused on unfamiliar material.

At the back of my mind the thing that embarrasses me slightly about my very early work is that because of my assumptions about the nature of the world I really thought I was writing about a world that was fairly whole. It took me a long time to see that I had no society to write about. I had to write differently. I had to look at the world afresh. It took a long time, it's very difficult. If you are trained by your reading and inclination to see the novel as one particular thing and if when you look at what you have, your material and you are aware only of its shallowness and its disorder, it's very hard to know how to move on from that.

But you have moved on, and although it may be true, as you once said, that you will never write social comedies about English middle-class life, none the less in a novel like The Mimic Men *you do penetrate whole areas, and important areas, of English society. Is this not so?*

It's probably just growing older. I began that book six years after writing that early article. But I think the problems about one's audience and one's material remain the same. Writing *is* essentially local, you know. One does need the response. One needs to have the exchange, otherwise it becomes such a private activity. I've got to accept this now, that it's totally private, that I'll never become a culture hero anywhere.

And yet it could be said that the England you have written about, the England as seen by the immigrant, is an England that most novel readers don't know much about. You don't feel any missionary impulse there—to reveal that England for us?

No. I think the difficulty about that is that probably every time you try to devise a story to get some kind of symbol for your experience the whole apparatus of invention that you'd have to bring to bear would be so fraudulent. How do you ceaselessly introduce the foreign character into a setting? You just can't go on doing that. That *is* very tedious and boring. This whole business of expatriate writing of having the expatriate figure in another culture, is one of the things, I realize now, which has separated me from a lot of the writing of this century. A lot of the English and American writing of this century. I've been trying a long time to define in my own mind why they always rejected me—I would say that, rather than that I rejected them. My thoughts clarified when I was extremely upset about this Bengal situation. My conclusions were that it wasn't a racial distinction because then you couldn't read books about any other culture except your own. Nor was it social, because the books that are most acceptable are those that pretend to deal, or do deal, with a totally created world—like, say, the comedies of Oscar Wilde. They don't reject you. Where one starts being rejected by this imperialist literature, as one must call it, is when this literature moves out of one protected, enclosed world and sets itself abroad, pretends it is having adventures and fails to see that it has assumed such security for itself.

Who do you have in mind? Kipling, Forster?

No, not Forster. No, I think *Passage to India* is about this, because Forster is always aware of the other side of the fence, Kipling is aware of the other side of the fence. Kipling is very much aware of the political realities of his world—brutally, accurately aware. No, I'm thinking of Hemingway, as an excellent example of a man who can go to a place like Paris, picture himself as an adventurer, writer, interested in sex and drink, and yet somehow never tell you what's going on in the streets outside. He reduces the whole of Paris in the 1920s and 1930s to someone trying to write. You see I cannot put myself in Hemingway's position because I know that in the 1930s someone like myself would never have been able to go to Paris like that. Do you see? So I am rejected at even that very simple level. Hemingway asks me to enter a kind of fairyland. An openly imperialist writer like Captain Marryat is less fraudulent, or less disingenuous. And you can say that writers like Kipling and Marryat made the world safe for Hemingway. There is a book called *When William Came* by Saki. It is a very interesting book. It was written in 1913. Now, I can accept the Saki of the short stories—there you do have the totally created society and the writer writes within it. And then Saki writes *When William Came*. This is a book about the defeat of England by the Germans. It's a mournful, passionate book about the disaster that will come. But what Saki does is that he visualizes England fighting back, a new spirit rising, and where is this new government set? It is set in India, a totally subjected land. So there you have this sort of moral blindness, that doesn't see one half of the world. And I am totally rejected by it. I can't enter into that feeling at all. And this is where one *cannot* be part of the tradition. I've spent a lot of time these last few years trying, as I say, to define why one felt out of it, one felt one didn't belong to this tradition of English letters. It was because its assumptions about the world were assumptions I could never make myself.

Do you feel you have an audience; or, rather, do you feel that in spite of this sense of not belonging, you do share an audience with Hemingway, that your readers are not likely to be essentially different from his?
I don't know where I have an audience. There are times when I do feel I'm just part of the English export trade.

I remember a columnist in The Times *saying, after you'd won the W. H. Smith award or something, "I wish we could give him more than prizes". As if we should try to cheer you up. Do you feel that there has been anything unpleasantly paternalistic in the fairly uniform enthusiasm with which your work has been received here? You are, I suppose, the most prize-laden novelist of recent years. How do you feel about all this official, as opposed to popular, response?*
I'm very touched by it. As I was saying earlier, without London, without the great generosity of people in London, of critics and editors, one would have been trying to write in a wilderness, without any sort of tradition behind *oneself*. It would have been an impossible occupation. So that has mattered to me, yes.

You talked earlier about the new security of the English. For security we might, presumably, read "complacency". You mentioned the chic interest in Black Power. What other symptoms would you name?

Well, another thing one feels out of here is the theatrical cause, literature of the theatrical cause. I can no longer, at a time of crisis, in Bengal, take an interest in plays which don't have a proper setting, where people are in a way symbols, where incidents are always symbolic, where people are endlessly looking for their doubles, or acting out old myths, or where plays are set in madhouses. There are too many plays set in madhouses. But I wonder how real this colonial attitude of the English is, how much of it is imposed. Newspapers like *The Times* or *The Sunday Times* have shown in the Bengal situation just how passionately concerned people here can be about important issues, but if this concern is to be frustrated by governments and civil servants who have decided that expediency is the only good, how much longer can such concern be generated? And if governments look on expediency as the only good, how can art, which is an expression of concern, exist? If expediency is the only good, there can be no discussion, and people will then forever live in a world where the only real causes are in America, and where if you are living in England you have nothing to write about. Therefore you must set your play in a madhouse. I can't accept that because I live in a world where too many things are happening. One is far too insecure. So there is this further separation. Politics—if you can all it that—may then divide us.

I notice that one whole section of your next novel, In a Free State, *is set in America, in Washington in fact, but that America is really very vague and distant. One is told of fires burning in the distance, and there is a general sense of violence in the air, but there is not a great deal of descriptive, or any other kind of detail.*

None at all, no, none at all. The immigrant's view of the capital of the world, the view of a man from another, enclosed culture. Rather like my own of London, twenty years ago. The view clears up but only in a limited way. Since I went to India I've become interested in the way different cultures have different ways of seeing. Columbus, a medieval man, voyaging in a miraculous world, which causes him no surprise. Isaac Newton living in both worlds. Gandhi coming to England and leaving not a word of description, remembering only that when he arrived at Southampton, he was dressed in white.

Is there any prospect of your going on from your new book, to make some "larger statement" about America?

None at all.

Well, I can't say I'm not relieved.

I think that whole section of *In a Free State* is in a way a comment on what I've been talking about.

Also in that book, in the long final section, you have as your main characters two middle-class English people, and you use a lot of middle-class English dialogue . . .

Yes, a lot of dialogue. There is no trouble for me in writing that sort of dialogue, none at all.

At one time, though, you would have said that this was precisely the sort of dialogue you couldn't handle, that you'd never get hold of the nerve of it, or feel close enough to it . . .

Yes, well, I've spoken to an awful lot of middle-class people since I said that. And the middle-class English characters you refer to are in Africa. I'm not sure that I could have managed them in their own setting.

I feel that the book offers a much grander, much more total, vision of placelessness than you've offered before. There is hardly a nationality that is not represented somewhere—there are Indians, Africans, Americans, but there are also Danes, Germans, Chinese, Swedes, and so on, and they are all of them on the move, they are all uprooted, "in a free state". In other words, the predicament, the lostness, is one we all share . . .

Absolutely. You see, one of the things that struck me, and has struck me for many years, is that even at the height of imperial power, even when people make the most fantastic assumptions about their place in the world, they still have these enormous personal problems, problems that can make their power seem meaningless to them, make it merely the background to their own anguish. That was one thing that's upset me, and then there is this new thing, which you have seen, that it's a recurring thing, that you do have English people who go to Africa, in search of some sort of personal fulfillment, and are lost, just as you have an Indian servant who goes to America and is lost. It's very hard for me to talk about my work in that way.

You say you don't want any more plays about madhouses, and I think I see what you mean. But you don't feel also that the categorizing impulse is a dangerous one, in the sense that to see people always in terms of rank and nationality might entail some sort of blindness to the conditions we all share, to the . . . well, to the threat of madness that we are all, at some deep level, subject to?

I don't think an interest in one necessarily involves a blindness to the other. The fact that people can be categorized politically, racially and socially, doesn't mean that one is unaware of them in the other way. I think that's the point of my book, in fact.

Yes, well, I certainly see it in this book in a way that I haven't always seen it in your other work.

In a way, I regard this book as a rather final statement on this thing really. But it has taken me such a long time to work towards that from that great sense of the oddity of people, in my early books. Then the lost individual, and now to this. It has been a great effort, it has required greater and greater understanding of the world, greater growing up.

Unfurnished Entrails—
The Novelist V. S. Naipaul
in Conversation with
Jim Douglas Henry

Jim Douglas Henry / 1971

From *The Listener*, 25 November 1971, 721. Reprinted by permission of Jim Douglas Henry.

In a letter to a friend, V. S. Naipaul said of his recently published In a Free State: *'I feel I've been lucky during the conceiving and the writing of this book. Lucky because I feel it's the book that this whole writing career was meant to lead up to.' How did luck come into it?*

I think that one has luck in all writing. One has luck right at the beginning when you are just starting to try to write. How difficult it is then to give your work authority. And then, after a lot of trial and error, one day a kind of miracle occurs. And the lines you write do have authority. You somehow have learnt to shape a paragraph a little bit more, and it's more than just a piece of prose. There's that character in Chekhov's play, *The Seagull*: they all talk about writing and they're all very wise about writing there, and one of these idle figures in the background tells the young man who's trying to write: 'Have an idea. Otherwise you won't be able to write, and you'll be destroyed by your talent.' You know, one has to stumble on this truth oneself. To have an idea. It's very hard to explain this; it's very hard to teach this to someone who is learning to write. But I've stumbled on it. I know what it means. And I was lucky. With every book there has been this element of luck, I feel, in the actual writing. You begin with very vague ideas. And the act of writing, or devising a story or form, is such an artificial thing: you have to woo life into this artificial thing—which doesn't even exist.

You are a born writer in the sense that Mozart was a born composer? He could compose before he could walk.

I'm afraid I don't think of myself as a born writer. I've learnt the very hard way.

When did you first think of yourself as being a writer? Did you want to be a writer before you wanted actually to write?

22

Absolutely. I think that's very much still with one. One is in love with the concept of being a writer. I suppose it probably goes back to my childhood. I used to see my father writing—my father tried to write and wrote stories. But until I was quite old I never even tried, because no miracle was occurring. I had nothing to write about. And I think one still feels like that: before a book, one is empty. 'Unfurnished entrails'—that was what Shaw said about himself when he was writing novels in the early days. One has to provide a book out of one's unfurnished entrails. One still has to do this wooing. If I say I was lucky with this book, I mean that as you get older there's so many more things to feel, so many more experiences that you can have. The promptings for a book are so manifold, and to find a kind of framework which will carry all the promptings and express them fully—that requires luck . . . Just to settle down and convert an idea into words on a page, and to let that have authority and life—I think that too requires an awful lot of luck. Particularly with this book, which is a book about journeys, unhappy journeys, by people switching countries, switching cultures.

What would have been the alternative for you in the West Indies, do you think, if you hadn't managed to become the writer you wished to be?
I saw myself as leaving the rather empty, barren place where I was born and rejoining the old world. It was as simple as that. Joining the real world again. I used to spend so much time trying to analyse why the world I was born in was not real. I used to think it was perhaps the light. There was something about the light that made it all unreal. For a long time I secretly believed this until I went to places like Egypt and Bihar in India where the light is very much like the light one knew but which have been centres of an enormous old civilisation. So it wasn't the light, but a sense of being in a wrong place. That society was such a simple one that I don't think there would have been room for me. I tried very hard when I left Oxford to get a job—to fit myself in. There was nothing I could do. So you might say that the mere fact that one turned to writing—the thing which one had thought of all of one's adolescence—and the fact that one had to turn to it rather seriously in order to create a career, this is probably a sign of the weakness of my own background.

V. S. Naipaul: A *Transition* Interview

Adrian Rowe-Evans / 1971

From *Transition* 40 (December 1971), 56–62. Reprinted by permission of *Transition* and Duke University Press.

Q: *Mr. Naipaul, the most overwhelming impression I get from your books is of a pursuit of honesty above all things. Is that a fair comment?*

Naipaul: I hope so. It's the impression one ought to get from serious writing. The wish to become a writer (which is how we all begin) has been brought about by our reading of other people, which gives us a vision of what a writer is. But then we have to find out what we want to do ourselves, what is our own voice; and that takes time. In my own case it took a lot of time. I had to go through a lot of writing, a lot of work, before I discovered what I really wanted, what I really felt, and how to trust my own reactions and not to prettify them in any way. So you have to discard the vision of yourself as 'a writer,' and find out what you want to say, and how you want to say it. For example, when I began reviewing in the *New Statesman* about thirteen years ago, my work was appalling, because I was trying to fill the *persona,* as I conceived it, of 'the reviewer,'—and I was writing rubbish. Until one day, in total despair, I tried just writing down what actually occurred in me when I read a particular book. It came out beautifully; the words seemed to write themselves and to sing—and people liked it. It was a great event, the discovery that it was myself and my own views that really mattered.

Q: *That was the start. But you were saying that it takes a long time. As you went on, did you feel that you were getting nearer to this honesty, this truth; and to being able to express it?*

Naipaul: Well yes; you have to. Otherwise you aren't really writing; you're falling into patterns. Even now I can often be seduced into applying a type of dramatic pattern to what I am portraying, so that I falsify the situation as I really perceive it. Or I might be seduced by the rhythm of the words themselves to say something which isn't really what I see. That's what one is fighting against all the time. On the other hand, if I react truly to a situation, I am reacting to what is true about it; I am discovering the truth about it.

Q: *Then you believe there is an objective truth?*

Naipaul: Yes. Provided that one takes everything into consideration, when one reacts to it.

Q: *Integrity? The whole personality reacting to the whole situation?*

Naipaul: Yes—you're not keeping anything back or glossing over anything or ignoring anything; you're trying to make a whole, an integrity, of it. You have to become adept in looking for the truth of your own responses. I think it's much more important for me, coming from a place which is not real, a place which is imperfectly made, and a place where people are, really, quite inferior, because they demand so little of themselves. They are colonials, in a type of perpetual colonial situation. Coming from such a society, I didn't really have views of my own; I didn't know what I thought about anything, because the world was out of my hands. So this establishing of a position, an intellectual stance, has come to me quite recently. In writing my first four or five books (including books which perhaps people think of as my big books) I was simply recording my reactions to the world; I hadn't come to any conclusion about it. (It was the reviewers who came to a conclusion!) But since then, through my writing, through the effort honestly to respond, I have begun to have ideas about the world. I have begun to analyse. First of all, the deficiencies of the society from which I came; and then, through that, what goes to make this much more complex society in which I have worked so long.

Q: *Is it an advantage, to begin in a simpler society?*

Naipaul: Well, there are two sides to that. But on balance it is a great disadvantage. A writer floats at the level of his society; you can't have a tree growing in a desert. In Trinidad, in my childhood, there wasn't even a proper general bookshop as you'd understand it. There was nothing like Criticism, naturally. You were doing it all yourself. So there was intellectual isolation, added to the commercial and practical disadvantage of not having an audience that will buy your books or support you as a writer. In that sort of country some people may feel that writing is an aspect of their political assertion, or an aspect of the tourist trade. But that has nothing to do with the real quality of life, or with the liveliness of the culture; it is no substitute for genuine cultural activity; the writer has no loving cultural world about him, and has to make his way into another world, one which is entirely alien to him. Imagine a writer like Dostoievski, trying to sell his work to, say, the Australians in 1865, and you'll get some idea. Well, when I began writing I believed in the Universality of Art—if one produced a work of art, then there would be universal recognition of it. Now I know that all art is local, a communication between the maker and the receiver of it. They must both have the same equipment.

Q: *In* The Mimic Men, *one of the characters tries to divide up the world's culture into three groups—those of long, medium and short vision.*

Naipaul: Yes, I remember. The people who are going to get things done are those of medium vision. The long-visioned ones, the people who had long vistas of eternity to play with, were so overwhelmed by all that that they weren't going to do much, whereas the short-visioned man, say the hunter in the South American bush who is going to kill an animal and eat it all at once, has no place in his thoughts for anything other than the immediate act.

Q: *Does that also mean that the medium-visioned man is more likely to deceive himself? The long-visioned man may be able to escape to a large extent from immediate circumstances and not react to them; he distinguishes completely between the act and the spirit. For the short-visioned man, pursuing his animal, the spirit and the act are the same thing. The medium-visioned man in getting so much done may be bound to compromise and muddle up the spirit and the facts, each for the sake of the other. In other words, the man of action has dirty hands—often bloody hands?*

Naipaul: No doubt. I often wish I could have been a doer. But then I do have a great distrust of *causes,* simply because they *are* causes and they have to simplify, to ignore so much. As a man of action one would be continually weakened by harking after the truth, by too-honestly reassessing the situation all the time; so that for example in Africa you can get a profound refusal to acknowledge the realities of the situation; people just push aside the real problems as if they had all been settled. As though the whole history of human deficiencies was entirely explained by an interlude of oppression and prejudice, which have now been removed; any remaining criticism being merely recurrence of prejudice and therefore to be dismissed.

Q: *But need all action lead to dishonesty? For example, writers seek their own truth; they describe it, they publish and they influence other people. Is that a form of action?*

Naipaul: One can only speak for oneself. I've gone through a great deal of anguish to achieve a certain kind of understanding of the world. If one could pass that one to one's readers, so that if, for example, one of them wanted to be a writer he could start working at a much higher level than I did, or could more easily avoid the sort of nonsensical ideas that I had—then one would feel one had acted, and feel rewarded.

Q: *You must surely have such a feeling. But there must be dangers in it, too; for instance, I've come across African writers who were altogether too anxious to develop 'African writing,' so that those who came after them could more easily be better 'African Writers.' I always felt they were mistaken.*

Naipaul: Why yes, it is a mistake. Of course there are good writers who are African. Chinua Achebe is a grand writer by most people's standards, but he is not published in his own country. His work needs the blessing of the foreign market, and for a very good reason; because the local society doesn't have any body of judgement as yet; it can't trust itself yet to make its own appraisals.

Q: *But surely that must come, eventually?*

Naipaul: I think it will be a long process. One of the terrible things about being a Colonial, as I have said, is that you must accept so many things as coming from a great wonderful source outside yourself and outside the people you know, outside the society you've grown up in. That can only be repaired by a sense of responsibility, which is what the colonial doesn't have. Responsibility for the other man. As a colonial, you must first seek to remove yourself from what you know, and become blest personally, before you can become responsible for others.

Q: *Are you laying too much stress on that? There are so many forms of dependence, and dependence always breeds irresponsibility. You don't feel that a writer brought up in an 'advanced' society can be equally dependent, and equally emasculated by dependence?*

Naipaul: Perhaps. But as I said before, a writer should have a dialogue with his own society, and to have writers who have got one eye on an exterior world is to use writers as a tourist trade, as a cultural or political weapon, and perhaps this is why so little of that kind of writing has made any impact. To write honestly about one's own undeveloped society would offend it; ten years ago in Trinidad, if you called an African black, the man was mortally offended. In those days many people were offended by my writings. Now, I get letters from tourist boards asking if my work can be used, and so forth. What future can there be for a kind of writing which can be treated, or used, like that?

Q: *All right. But it isn't only Africans who abuse African writers. There are plenty of people, literary people, in this country who say to them: "Please do something absolutely African! Bring a new stream into our culture, wake us up, make us sexually alive or something of the kind; we are short of something we think you might have; please tell us what it is!"*

Naipaul: Well, yes. But I think not many people set up that cry.

Intelligent people, people of refined intellect, are always looking for
writers who will help them to place themselves in the world. And they
won't get that sort of help from the sort of self-conscious 'African
Writing' which is obsessed with tribal *mores,* for instance. Yet that is part
of the trap in which Africa has found itself; a lot of this writing is being
encouraged by publishers who have London bases, who are hoping to
exploit a new market. They are publishing work on London presses,
which wouldn't stand a chance in the regular market. Cotton goods for
the natives. And I think it's being promoted by a kind of salesman who
thinks he understands the native.

Q: *Neo-colonial?*

Naipaul: Certainly. Because that seems to be one of Africa's funda-
mental functions—to keep on being a perpetual colony; a little treasure-
house; a playground for people who want a play-culture, a play-industry;
a play development.

Q: *I think you're right. Even the Romans, so long ago said* Ex Africa
semper aliquid novi—*a new thing, not in the intellectual sense, but in the
sense of a plaything, a conversation-piece, something amusing and
strange?*

Naipaul: Yes. And I find that I have no desire to understand Africa in
that way. I don't want to be given descriptions of exotic manners; I want
writing, somehow, to light up my position as a fairly educated man who
has thought a lot about the world in the twentieth century. If people think
that something cruder is needed, then they are greatly mistaken. On the
contrary, a greater depth and subtlety is needed, and I wonder whether it
could come from the Africa of today. We want more realism, not more
romanticism; the time for that is finished. When I was in East Africa
recently, I was constantly hearing on every side that this was the Decade
of Africa, as if Africa were suddenly going to become technically,
educationally, culturally advanced, and politically powerful. I was appalled to find that people who possessed a few tiny skills were so
convinced that they, simple people, were carrying the seeds of all
civilisation, all culture, all literature, all technology. That was rubbish. If
you buy a typewriter made in Germany and, using Swedish paper, type
out a story in English, which you then submit to a London paper—how
can you regard yourself as a local writer? The idea that all the things
which have been presented to Africa have somehow been already assimi-
lated and appropriated by Africa, is the most hideous type of conning. It
may be a willing conning, voluntary on both sides, but it remains conning.

Q: *But what is the alternative? What should I do, if I'm an African
and I feel the urge to write?*

Naipaul: It's easier to say what he shouldn't do. I do feel, very strongly, that Art is one and indivisible, and there is no point in a writer, whether he comes from Africa or anywhere else, doing today what Dickens or Tolstoy did a hundred years ago. African writers can't cover all that ground again. On the other hand, to encourage a young man merely to write nostalgically about tribal life is really slightly ridiculous. A man must write to report his whole response to the world; not because it would be nice to do something for the prestige of his country.

Q: *So the dilemma is rather like the political one. You said somewhere, speaking of political action, that it is the very reason which makes the political movement possible, which also makes it futile. The fact that you can succeed along these lines, destroys the very meaning of success.*

Naipaul: Yes. Revolutions can come about very easily in undeveloped societies, precisely because there is so little understanding of the society even as it is; so little intellectual base. And of course for that reason, the result of the revolution is nothing. Nothing has changed; the deficiencies remain, they remain un-analysed; and the response is the same; the march, the borrowed ideas, the refusal to understand what makes a whole society—or a whole world.

Q: *What about the coming generations? You wrote once about the particular dishonesties of youth: its pathetic eagerness to embrace the apparent solution, the sham idea.*

Naipaul: You mean in Universities? Yes; when they join political movements one suspects it's just part of pretending to be adult, pretending to be responsible, pretending to be grown-up.

Q: *Well, there's a terrible irony about student life nowadays. On the one hand, you're trying hard to develop your mind, to widen its grasp, to make understanding more complex and subtle. On the other, you must have answers now, simple answers which will give you the power, the passion, that you hope will make a grown man of you. You can't grow up, in fact, because you too desperately want to.*

Naipaul: Yes. And then you get the creation of the myths, which people will cling to, however absurd they are. Take a place like Trinidad, where they talk about Black Power and appear to believe in the ridiculous idea that there is somehow a great movement in the world, for black people only. It's a kind of hysteria, which can happen easily enough in places where people feel that they are on the other side of the real world. You do, from time to time, get these movements which promise Jerusalem. In about 1836 there was an ex-slave, called Daga, who thought he would walk back across the Atlantic Ocean to Africa; and he did have a little following; there was a mutiny that was quelled. A hundred years

later there was a sort of holy man who formed a movement, created a
strike in the oil-fields—and again Jerusalem didn't come. Then, more
recently, you had Dr. Eric Williams, operating at an entirely different
level, introducing people to politics and the hope of political redemption.
Now, fourteen years later, it's Black Power, offering salvation again. The
hysteria recurs, but the situation doesn't change. Black Power is a great
mirage, and I fear it will end badly.

Q: *Harsh words. Yet I can't think of you as a harsh person; for me,
gentleness pervades your work. You are gentle to your characters, and
gentleness is one way of finding out the truth about them. On the other
hand you do want the truth, and that implies a certain ruthlessness. Is
there a conflict between the loving approach and what one might call the
surgical approach to character?*

Naipaul: Interesting question. One can't be entirely sympathetic; one
must have views; one must do more than merely respond emotionally. I
can get angry, impatient, like anyone else; I can be irritated, bored—but
you can't turn any of that into writing. So you have to make a conscious
effort to render your emotions into something which is more logical,
which makes more sense, but which is more, and not less, true. But
although you can't use the shallower emotions they are of great value in
getting you started. I may sit down in enormous rage to write something;
I might even begin in terms of caricature and animosity; but in the course
of writing, something will happen. That side of me, that comes out in the
writing, is the better side, and better not because it's nicer, but because
it's truer; it's the side that in one's rage one might wish to forget. I began
my recent book about Africa with a great hatred of everyone, of the
entire continent; and that had to be refined away, giving place to comprehension. If one wasn't angry, wasn't upset, one wouldn't want to write.
On the other hand it isn't possible to get anything down until you've
made sense of it, made a whole of it. To write one has to use all the
senses; all the pores must be open.

Q: *Then you see writing as a refining, perfecting process. Do you
believe in human perfectibility—are you an optimist?*

Naipaul: I'm not sure. I think I do like to look for the seeds of
regeneration in a situation; I long to find what is good and hopeful and
really do hope that by the most brutal sort of analysis one is possibly
opening up the situation to some sort of action; an action which is not
based on self-deception.

Q: *Your books do, I think, show a faith in humanity. You seem to be
able to approach all characters without fear, and fear is what distorts*

and depresses people's writing, as well as their lives. Does fear play no part in your life?

Naipaul: Well, you know, the nature of the life which I have imposed on myself has been one of physical non-involvement. I have never had to work for hire; I made a vow at an early age never to work, never to become involved with people in that way. That has given me a freedom from people, from entanglements, from rivalries, from competition. I have no enemies, no rivals, no masters; I fear no one. I used to have a sense of doom, which is not like fear; an irrational feeling of disaster about to come. But if a writer comes to fearing a principle, or a kind of person, which he thinks is inimical to him, it must of course upset his writing. I think it is this fear which underlies a good deal of what is called satire, or the attempt to be contemptuous of what you fear. That can't be done; rather you will be contemptuous of what you love, and exalt what you fear. That is particularly true of a lot of American writing. But I have been spared that particular kind of distortion. I come from a small society; I was aware that I had no influence in the world; I was apart from it. And then I belonged to a minority group, I moved away, became a foreigner, became a writer; you see the degrees of removal from direct involvement, from direct fear.

Q: *I wonder how far the achievement of a comprehensive world-view tends to cast out fear? Perfect knowledge; or perfect love, as the Bible puts it; casteth out fear. But that might well lead to another kind of fear—the sense of doom you mentioned; the fear of the disintegration of the familiar structure. Our world-views, our patterns of life, get out of date, and then we look to the artist to re-compose them; to make a new pattern which is somehow continuous with the old one.*

Naipaul: Yes. One must make a pattern of one's observations, one's daily distress; one's daily knowledge of homelessness, placelessness; one's lack of representation in the world; one's lack of status. These, for me, are not just ideas; when I talk about being an exile or a refugee I'm not just using a metaphor, I'm speaking literally. If daily one lives with this, then daily one has to incorporate the experience into something bigger. Because one doesn't have a side, doesn't have a country, doesn't have a community; one is entirely an individual. A person in this position risks going mad; I have seen it happen to others—it is a bizarre and frightening thing, and it is one of the great strands in my own writing. I long to be happy, I still have a great instinct towards great happiness and delight and pleasure. And the idea was that the work would absorb and obliterate all my distress, continually. At first I looked for this release in humour, but as the horizon of my writing expanded I sought to reconstruct my disintegrated society, to impose order on the world, to seek patterns, to tell myself—this is what happens when people are strong; this is what happens when people are weak. I had to find that degree of intellectual comfort, or I would have gone mad.

Q: *But surely everyone has to recreate the world for himself? Even someone whose background seems very intelligible and constant?*

Naipaul: Perhaps. I really cannot enter into the mind of a person for whom the world seems intelligible and constant; to whom their own situation appears normal and common. I think they too must have difficulty in understanding my work—for example many people in this country seem to think that when I am writing about, say Trinidad, I am writing about a society which is a quaint version of their own, with all its order and its regularities. Very few people in any kind of society can see anything except in terms of their own society. But it is worse in a society which is so culturally undeveloped and depressed, that people can't even see things in terms of their own society, because that society is not a coherent, understandable thing. Yet someone like myself, who has developed this gift in another place and is now trying to express the problem of his own background, will be speaking in a way that the man at home simply cannot follow.

Q: *I can't help being reminded of the same sentiments being expressed by writers who came from provincial backgrounds in England—say D. H. Lawrence or Wells.*

Naipaul: Colonial places are less than provincial. The province, you see, implies the existence of the metropolis; access to it, a partaking of the culture, the wealth, the political life of the metropolis, in however remote a way. In the colonial situation, one has only the most fleeing of glimpses.

Q: *But is it really different? In your own case, you had to adopt, to write from the metropolitan point of view. Yet you have built up an enormous admiration and respect, in this country, for your work. One feels that your readers must have more than a superficial knowledge of what you are talking about. Isn't it true that every human being, in the deepest psychological sense, is an exile in the world; that he is oppressed by the incoherence of the world, and the futility of trying to understand, or to be understood? And isn't that the starting-point of all great writers, wherever they come from?*

Naipaul: That may be so. But in many practical ways, things are harder for the writer who comes from an undeveloped society. Apart from the sheer difficulty of getting away, in order to get started at all. I can't help thinking that I might have had much greater success, been much better

understood as a writer, if I had been born in England. As it is, one has no
cultural attaches in a hundred countries pushing one's work. If I *have* a
reputation in England, well, it has taken a long time. I have been writing
now for more than sixteen years. I have done nothing else. It has been a
life's dedication, and I think an American, even a British, French,
German writer, would scoff at the rewards I have received. I don't mean
only in money, either; I am concerned about the dignity of myself as a
writer, and when I find people offending the status of my writing I can
get very angry. I have to protect that status, because there's no one
protecting it for me.

Q: *Of course, you must feel entirely responsible for the protection of
your work, because it is art, as well as for any other reason. And I have
noticed that even people like yourself, who are of great and assured
stature, can never feel in their hearts secure in that stature.*

Naipaul: No. Writers can never really know where they stand. How
can you know? You do your work; you do it over long periods of total
isolation; in the end you get your notices and your royalty statements,
and apart from that, you know, nothing. It's a rather horrible life, you
know; you can become awfully self-centered, and you get easily perturbed. You become crankish—I used to wonder why the writers I got to
know were all so crankish. I understand more and more; it's the sheer
solitude and loneliness of the job! They all long for human contact; they
want to see people, to be in touch with people who are reading their
work. And in a writer's life that's almost impossible. I've just been talking
to someone, someone young, who does a little writing, and I was trying
to analyse the difference between myself and her. I think it is that my
panic is always greater than hers—and all my work begins in panic.
Which she, maybe, can only simulate. But with me it's entirely real and
lasts for a long time. It's a feeling you can't communicate, explain to
other people; you can assuage it only by starting to write, even though
your mind is as blank as the next man's; you have no consciousness of
anything you want to say. And then, given the panic, the next thing you
need is a certain fortitude, a tenacity, to carry on through all the ups and
downs. They are very painful, these downs that can hit you even when
the work is quite advanced, and you have been practicing for a long time.
They can last for years, literally; and the only cure is to lever yourself
out of it, bodily, by sheer work. And sheer luck—you need luck all
the time.

Q: *So you begin with panic. Then you need guts to keep going, and
even then you won't get there unless you're lucky.*

Naipaul: Yes. Look at the book I've just finished. Such a strange process. It came out of this great panic; it went on in this enormous pain and anguish for months and months. It took fourteen months to write, and in that time I did nothing else except two articles. And yet, now that it's over I feel, as I feel about all of my work, that in a way I was not really responsible. I feel I was just a little vessel into which the thing was gradually and painfully distilled. In the end I just feel responsible for judgement, not the gifts of imagination and language; I feel that many fortuitous things have conspired to produce those gifts; all that is out of my hands.

Q: *Are you saying that the writing and the judgement of it are entirely separate processes? That they are almost being carried out by separate people?*

Naipaul: Not quite. If one could feel that the judging process was completely austere and objective, that would be wonderful. But it isn't quite so. In all my work, in all my life, I will always be dependent on outside opinion and encouragement. In the early stages of any piece of work I have no idea of the value of anything I am writing, and I need to be told: "It's good—you must go on!" Sometimes I don't go on, because I really know it's bad. Even when it isn't, there are lots of false starts and disappointments. Within oneself, both the executant and the judge become very tired, dispirited; one longs for more help, support, encouragement. Then, towards the end, even that's no good; everything depends on working, holding on, husbanding your slender resources of energy. You're on your own, then. You feel threatened; every distraction, every single thing, can lessen your creative capacity. You have to be so very careful, over the last few months.

Q: *Carrying this vessel with extreme care. You make it seem an anxious, painful, laborious life. Do you sometimes want to get away from it, or can you not imagine a life that was not writing?*

Naipaul: Oh, yes! About ten years ago, when I was going through a time of really monstrous labour which extended over nearly three years; my biggest book; I used to console myself with that fantasy. I would imagine that a man would come to me and say, I'll give you a million pounds, if only you will stop writing; you must not finish this book. But I knew I would have to say, No. Well, today I wouldn't say no. I've changed. As you get older you begin to write more profoundly; you are thinking less of the way the words lie on the paper, and more of the meanings, the timing, the emphasis—not thinking of style or language at all; just the effect. That has been my concern for so long; to achieve a writing which is perfectly *transparent*.

Q: *Isn't that perhaps simply the result of developing skill, of mastery?*

Naipaul: No. I know now that I can always write, turn out a good paragraph. But the result is that I am more concerned with thought, meaning, philosophy. Having discovered and then overcome the great difficulty of writing, one is confronted with the intractable nature of truth, the difficulty of one's own position, the utility of expression, the absence of reward for art, and the fact that all one is now really seeking; a true communication with a society; is non-existent and impossible. Having discovered that in absolute terms there is a great hollowness in my endeavor I might be prepared to give it up—I might even do it easily. But yet, paradoxically, I do retain a real concern for the dignity of my past work. I would like that to remain as it was done; to do nothing that would in any way belittle it. I would not like to start writing for the sake of money. If it could be done, I would like just to go silent; there have been many writers who, after a great success, have just gone silent. They are without the panic. And the early unspecific promptings to create a work of art, of wanting to be a writer, of wishing to be famous; they have all gone as well. Writing has become a much more practical business; communication of ideas; one's ambition has grown up into a simple desire to help—to serve.

Q: *But in your own case there can be no question that you help, you serve. There's the work, it does influence people, it illuminates their lives, the service continues. You are almost saying that the body of your accomplished work has an independent existence now; it is something which you can look at apart from yourself. You can think of its future, apart from your own future.*

Naipaul: Yes. I've lost both the arrogance and the humility that I once had. When I was young, I suppose the only people I really worshipped and adored were rich people, and writers. I no longer worship the rich, and I now respect writers; enormously respect them; but I don't worship them. I remember, in those days, seeing people like Joyce Carey at Oxford. They seemed magical men, and I just stared at them. Magic, magic, magic. But now, having known the sheer labour of the work, the hours that go into it, and the years; the trials and failures that nobody sees; I am left with respect, for their work and my own.

Q: *When you speak of your respect for writers, how wide is that term? Would it include people who are not novelists, who deal in smaller forms? Poets, for example?*

Naipaul: Well, I began with the simple idea of the writer as the creator of the work of art. That is something I have moved away from, now. There is the other idea of the writer as the communicator; the molder, rather than the man of imagination, and that is what interests me now. I suppose that doesn't mean that there is no place for imagination to play in literature. I used to be very humble about poetry, I felt that because my background had been deficient there was something there that I didn't, couldn't, understand. Now I feel that most people called poets are tiny people, with tiny thoughts. I don't like technical virtuosity, and I am not interested in trivial. Again, I admire journalism; a strong and immediate response to the world; I admire it in principle but in practice I can't say that I have ever looked at any journalist with the kind of respect that I feel for a great writer; the magician figure, the wise man.

Q: *Do you think the whole future of the novel, as well as your own future as a novelist, will be tending further away from the romantic, the imaginative function?*

Naipaul: Yes, I do. You might go on endlessly writing 'creative' novels, if you believed that the framework of an ordered society exists, so that after a disturbance there is calm, and all crises fall back into that great underlying calm. But that no longer exists for most people, so that kind of imaginative work is of less and less use to them. They live in a disordered and fast-changing world, and they need help in grasping it, understanding it, controlling it. And that is how the writer will serve them.

Fame, A Short-Lived Cycle, Says Vidia

Eric Roach / 1972

From *Trinidad Guardian,* 4 January 1972, 1–2. Reprinted by permission of Trinidad Guardian Co.

Trinidad yesterday informally welcomed home one of its most distinguished sons, writer Vidia Naipaul, who has returned to spend a holiday of undetermined length.

His stay would be determined by the conclusion of arrangements to go to Brazil to write an article about that country for a newspaper, he said.

Naipaul said he has not worked seriously, except for a couple of newspaper articles, since the conclusion (about 14 months ago) of his award winning work *In a Free State.* He has not been well for some time.

Asked how he felt to be a lion among literary men in Britain, he said that fame is a short-lived cycle bringing the sort of popularity and corruption from which he was glad to escape for the moment. However, he was rather delighted about the economic side of it because beside the prize itself, the book has sold so much better since it was announced that he won the $24,000 on Booker award (Britain's most prestigious in the literary field) and trophy.

In a wide-ranging Press interview at Stephens, Frederick Street, Port-of-Spain, Naipaul expressed his views on West Indian writing, the emanation of "black power," the nature of Third World societies and his own progress as a writer. The majority of his comments were induced by questions put to him by the media.

He said his latest book was influenced by his own feelings of estrangement and loneliness experienced in different communities. But he has, as yet, no solutions to his personal problem of being a sojourner and disinterested observer everywhere he goes.

He feels the solution is in earning as much as he can in order to enjoy a comfortable retirement somewhere when he could no longer write.

Speaking of 1970 in Trinidad "and all that," Naipaul said he thought "black power" could create anarchy, that it carried a kind of pre-colonial feebleness, so that the whole imperial cycle might quite easily start all over again.

He linked "black power" uprisings to the Daaga revolt a century ago and to the Butler riots in 1937. What is disappointing about the "black power" manifestations is that its "intellectual bases seem to be so fragile." "I find it very hard to come to terms with something which has a negligible intellectual content."

He added that "black power" adherents always talked in vague abstractions. They had no idea of the weakness of the unskilled in the modern worlds.

"The creation of true power is a very complex, slow, painful thing. It depends on a lot of hard work. It depends on a lot of people quietly practicing lots of skills—new skills undoubtedly."

The history of black countries in the post-colonial era is such a disastrous history because there is no concern about what power really is: They have no conception of what really makes a country. No one ever talks about it. Nobody ever discusses it. "These countries aren't supported by thought or thinkers even where real issues are beaten out."

In his view, Trinidad cannot be classified as a developed nor a developing country and probably cannot become a real solid country "like countries we know."

He does not see it as an under-developed country either, because we have an educated and fairly advanced consumer society. "It is a curious state that people in Trinidad are in," he said.

About the physical development of Port-of-Spain, he said: "I have no right to talk about these things."

He said he is "greatly disturbed" by the eastern section of Port-of-Spain. He regards it as an aesthetic collapse which wounds him more than lack of economic development. The new housing developments are "very distressing. They lie like lead on my spirit."

"It's Every Man for Himself"—
V. S. Naipaul on India

Charles Wheeler / 1977

From *The Listener*, 27 October 1977, 535, 537. Reprinted by permission of Charles Wheeler.

Charles Wheeler: *Mr. Naipaul, can I ask you first about the title of your book,* India: A Wounded Civilisation *(Deutsch £3.95)? My first impression is that 'wounded' is possibly an understatement—that your view is, rather, that it's a dying civilisation, if not a deservedly dead one. Is that unfair?*

V. S. Naipaul: You can't say that it's dead because it's still as it were, conditioning the responses of people in India. When I say 'wounded,' I think I mean this is a civilisation that is so damaged by invasions, and all the death and destruction that went with those invasions, that the people have had to adapt what was once a living civilisation to the fact of defeat, to the fact of intellectual depletion.

Do you feel, when you look at present-day India, that all this should be swept away, and something new should take its place?

I don't think things can be swept away. What I would like to see, not only in India but in other parts of the world as well, is a more cogent, a more lucid play of mind. I would like to see people getting away from an unexpressed faith in magic. A play of mind would mean opening oneself to the outside world—opening oneself to inquiry of all sorts, asking about history, getting some sense of time, getting some sense of what links men together, getting some sense of human contract. I think India at the moment is so far from these things that its attempts to become a modern country are slightly mimic attempts. You get the impression, when you read Indians' attempts to analyse their situation, that they are mimicking other people's intellectual disciplines. When you read a work of Indian history, you don't feel that there has been a true comprehension of Indian history. You feel that what the people have done is to study the way European history has been written, and to apply this method to the events of India, which are quite distinct, after all, from the events of Europe. Europe can look back to a continuous human development, especially over the last 1,000 years, perhaps. India can only look back to a series of stops and starts. And for Indians to pretend that this can be analysed in the way that Europe can be analysed is nonsense.

You seem to me to be asking for almost more than that, for a sort of regeneration. Do you think the changes that you want can be built on what is there?

I don't think they can be built on what is there, because what is there is really very, very disagreeable. What is there teaches man that you must look after yourself, then you must look after your family, then you look after your clan or your caste or tribe. There is no sense of responsibility of man for man outside these petty groupings. And I think these narrow loyalties come from great insecurity. They come from the many layers of which India is made up—all the people who have come into India at different times. I would like Indians to break out of these very restricted attitudes to their fellow men, and see men as their fellows.

But alas! The whole course of the independence struggle was governed by an idea of India recovering its past, its pre-British past. And to many people this simply meant going back proclaiming the past, however defeated, however narrow. The independence struggle bred some rather fine men with large views, but these great men, and these big views, were really a response to Western civilisation as people saw it in India. Now that the British presence is no longer there, what you are seeing in India—what you are seeing very clearly now after the overthrow of Mrs. Gandhi—is an awakening of a very old, very village, very petty India, that really has lost its way. I think that we are seeing now people to whom India is not even an idea that they can manage. They don't know what their country is. They just know what their little regions are, what their families are, what their clans or castes see.

You're surely not saying that this decline has occurred in the past three months? It must have been going on for hundreds of years.

No, this particular decline was built into the independence struggle, which proclaimed the Indian past, and the virtues of the past. Now you're getting the backlash of that proclamation. You're getting men saying: 'I want to be prime minister because I get up in the morning and spin my spinning wheel. I'm a Gandhian. This makes me a suitable man.' This is nonsense. The lies that have been put forward during this emergency, and since, have really been quite staggering. For example, a lot of the opposition to Mrs. Gandhi was so-called 'Gandhian'. The election was fought, I believe, on the plea that India should get back to the Gandhian economic system. No one knows what that means. And, of course, this is nonsense. You have people at the same time now going around talking about the need to get more machine tools from Europe or the need to export more engineering products. You have these constant contradictions in India—the simple past, the pre-industrial past, the holy past, the religious past, the spinning wheel past—and yet the need to meet the needs of a restless and growing population.

When you go to India, do you regard it as partly your country? Do you have these rather anguished feelings about India, as an Indian?
I used to.

You seem less detached than most foreigners, I mean people like me, Westerners, who can also be angry and irritated by India, but who don't have quite this same anguished sense that you appear to have in your book.
Well, you see, I am of Indian ancestry, and I think at quite an early age I understood that what was very important about a person in the world was not really his individual quality, but his political status, what kind of flag he had. I come from a very small community in a rather backward part of the world. And I wanted to join the big world, and I discovered I had no flag. So I had a concern for India. But, alas, this has really been beaten out of me during all these years that I've been taking an interest in India. I have picked up the Indian message—it's every man for himself, and his family.

What kind of society did you expect to find, when you came from your little corner of India in Trinidad, and went across this vast distance, this huge, milling country?
If you come from an overseas community, you are described as, say, an Indian. You are given a kind of racial grouping, and you grow up with this, because everybody has a racial grouping in certain parts of the world. And you go to India, and you find that there is no such feeling in India, that there is no sense not only of a racial grouping, but no sense of a country. It does rather leave you floating a little. That was my great, great disappointment, as you might say.

It was a political shock as much as anything, was it?
A political shock, yes. And I see it now as a great, great weakness of India—that men who really understand only the village and the caste can have no concept of a country, can have no concept of what a country needs.

I don't think the word 'Hinduism' has cropped up in our conversation, and yet the book is full of it. Do you reject Hinduism entirely, or is it just

*certain aspects of Hinduism that revolt you: for example, the caste
system?*

For me, Hinduism is a link with the past, a link with the classical
world, if you wish. So that is very much part of one's background, part
of one's heritage. But I must apply my mind to its practices. I must apply
my mind to its speculation. I have to admit, at the same time, that a lot
of Hindu attitudes, the deeper attitudes, are probably also mine—that I
probably do have a feeling about the vanity of human action and human
life. I have developed a kind of speculative mind which is leading me into
very strange and fairly disquieting paths now. I'm trying to control it. I
regard it as part of my bad blood coming to the surface when I start
playing with ideas of time and space.

*To take a particular thing, you talk about the way Hinduism perpetu-
ates the passive acceptance of intolerable conditions. Don't you think,
possibly, it is just as well, in the circumstances, that Hinduism does do
that, when you look at the lot of the peasant in India, and the chances of
anything materially changing in his lifetime?*

Well, that is one way of looking at it; but I think, you see, that it also
ensures that there will be no change—the acceptance of that attitude,
that what we see is a reflection of man's past life, and a man is being
punished for the sins of a past life. Even if you do take the Hindu idea,
that men have to express themselves, you'll see that men really need to
express all the senses, all their capacities. And you would feel that men
are being crippled, even if you accept the full Hindu thing.

*Your attitude to the emergency interested me. I got the impression
from your book—though I don't think you'd quite made up your mind—
that you were not unsympathetic to Mrs. Gandhi's action—that you
thought perhaps a dose of discipline was what the country needed.*

I was not unsympathetic to Mrs. Gandhi, and I remain not unsympathetic to her, largely because when I went to India I was appalled by the
opposition people. I was appalled by their intellectual negligibility, I was
appalled by the lies. I was later appalled by many aspects of the opposition overseas to Mrs. Gandhi, because some of those organisations were
not really reputable, and they had slightly grotesque aims which they
concealed in their plea for democracy. I also think that Mrs. Gandhi
might be considered the last of the great all-India leaders.

*What about the lies that were told by her government during the
emergency? I don't want to get into a political discussion, but it does
seem to me that the election showed, on the part of the people of India,*

*a fairly strong revulsion against the emergency. Why do you think there
was a huge majority against Mrs. Gandhi in the last election? Doesn't
that undermine, to some extent, your belief that Hinduism encourages
this passive acceptance of intolerable conditions?*

I would be very heartening if that were so. But I think that the election
results do not have that simple explanation only. In 1971, Mrs. Gandhi
split the Congress party and took over, won the structure, the machine in
many places. And what happened some months ago was that she simply
lost that machine. I don't think it had to do, in many places, with popular
resentment. It had to do with people walking away from her, people in a
big state of Uttar Pradesh, just saying: 'No, we're on the other side.'
Because I think that the structure of power in India remains quite intact.

*You have written a book that is not a novel, that is an analysis. Are
you drifting towards journalism now, in your approach to India?*

No, no, no. In fact, the book probably marks the end of that. I write a
novel about every four years. I regard the novel writing as engaging the
truer part of me. This doesn't mean that I don't take what I do in non-
fiction seriously. I take it very seriously, this part of my work. But this is
the end. The book was very exhausting to write, this analysis, this
shaping of chapters. I was unwilling always to describe simply; I always
try to make description part of an argument. I've spent all this year trying
to wash myself clean of this. I want to go back to imagination. I want to
stay here. It doesn't mark the beginning, it marks the end.

*What is your opinion of Indian novelists writing today? For example,
you talk quite a lot in your book about R. K. Narayan. You say that he
writes about small people in a small world.*

I'll explain a little bit about Narayan. He is very interesting in showing
how Indians, when they take a Western form, have some trouble with it.
The form of the novel implies concern with the condition of men.
Narayan's message in all his books is that the condition of men is not
important. So there is this oddity—writing about people as though human
life matters, and the deeper pessimistic rejection of a concern with men.
This makes Narayan's novels slightly odd to me. I find with the other
Indian novelists that I've read that they are people who experience,
because of religion and caste and all the attitudes that caste breeds, a
restriction of vision. They regard writing as a form of autobiography and
boasting, and I think it is this boasting aspect of Indian writing that
distresses me. I don't think Indians quite understand what the novel is
for. They do not quite accept that it has to do with a concern with human
existence. How can you—if all your philosophy, all your deeper attitudes
tell you that human existence is a dream?

When you go back to India after writing a book of this kind, are you conscious of Indian sensibility, their readiness to take offence, their deep feelings about foreign criticism? Does it inhibit you in your writing?

No, it doesn't inhibit me, for several reasons. One is that I think unless one hears a little squeal of pain after one's done some writing one has not really done much. That is my gauge of whether I have hit something true. Also, in India, I find that the people who respond violently usually haven't read the books. And I no longer forgive this. When I was younger, I would forgive this. Being an Indian ancestrally does give me a greater and greater liberty. And, in fact, when people say 'This book is so pessimistic', my attitude now is 'But it can't be pessimistic, because I have written it.' And by that I mean I am ancestrally of the culture—so the fact that I have written it might be taken as a sign of a mind at work.

Tell me, where do you feel at home?

I'm beginning to feel more and more at home in England, after 27 years. I came to England in 1950 and about eight years afterwards began to feel a little restless here. And this restlessness persisted until a few months ago. I really feel quite at home here now.

Are you going to stay in Britain, make this your home?

I think I'll stay here.

What is it about British society that you like? You're very critical of some societies—obviously India.

I think it's that people here have worked out a good way—perhaps the best way—of men getting on with men. I think there is a wonderful sense of human rights and human needs here.

You don't see this as a class-ridden society as you see India as a caste-ridden society?

Oh, there is class, but it works both ways. You know, if you stay a lot in the country, as I do, you find that there are many forms of indestructible pride, on both sides.

Meeting V. S. Naipaul

Elizabeth Hardwick / 1979

From *New York Times Book Review*, 13 May 1979, 1, 36.
Reprinted by permission of Elizabeth Hardwick.

On our way to Brazil in 1962, we stopped for some time in Trinidad. We did not meet V. S. Naipaul until a few years later, but we were led to his brilliant early novel, *A House for Mr. Biswas*. So, from the first his genius was clear. It is now 22 years and 14 books since he began, and Naipaul is still in his 40s.

It has come about that this writer, who at the beginning might have appeared in unique occupation of a marginal and peripheral world, is instead writing from the center of a historical vicissitude, utterly contemporary. His vision is fixed upon the brutal collision of cultures, the elaborate paralysis of "areas of darkness" and "wounded civilizations," phrases used as the titles of his books on India. Now, he has passed beyond India, or at least the land mass of India, to a universal "darkness." Talking to him, reading and re-reading his work, one cannot help but think of a literal yesterday and today, of Idi Amin, the Ayatollah Khomeini, of the fate of Bhutto. These figures of an improbable and deranging transition come to mind because Naipaul's work is a creative reflection upon a devastating lack of historical preparation, upon the anguish of whole countries and peoples unable to cope.

His own pedigree, if it may be named in that way, reads like an old map with its antique trade routes. His ancestors came from an ancient Asian civilization, India, and he was born in the new world of Trinidad. And what is he now—English? Yes, if the refined lucidity of his prose is a measure. England is where he lives and where he does his writing. "I do not write for Indians," he says, "who in any case do not read. My work is only possible in a liberal, civilized Western country. It is not possible in primitive societies."

There is nothing tropical or picturesque in Naipaul's fiction, even though the scenic, the external shape of Africa or India inhabits the books, acting as a sort of deceiving hieroglyph for visitors from the foreign world. His landscape is very old—Anglo-Africa and French Africa, South America, India, the Caribbean—but he approaches these crippled cultures alert to the deceits of their mythology, so much of it literary.

"I have visions of Central Asian horsemen, among whom I am one, riding below a sky threatening to snow to the very end of an empty world." This passage from the beautiful novel *The Mimic Men* at times seems to me to describe Naipaul himself. Except that horsemen do not have need of the severe and yet gleaming intelligence, the daring and rather dangerous wit of the "Asian horseman" who has written the books.

The complexity of Naipaul's novels lies in their balance of negative forces, or perhaps one should say in their balance of negative dreams, since everyone—African, Indian, Englishman—is *acting out*, that is, playing that part assigned to him in his meeting with those of a different past, acting out without regard for the reality of the part assigned.

On the surface, the novels are very clear, open. They are inventive with narrative, respectful of it; and populated by vivid, "global" characters. "What I am doing is sufficiently painful and novel to have no need of structural deformations," he explains, although I would not agree in the face of the radical and successful structure of *In a Free State*.

In the classical sense, the novels are comedies. Yet they are in no way comedies of the colonial mind, touching down here and there, looking for a fantastic and pedantic colorfulness. Naipaul's novels are comedies of a peculiarly modern pretension. Pretension trying to float above its own ignorance, fear and confusion as it expresses itself in dialogue, commands, apologies: all of the language of an eloquent misapprehension. "What I have in mind," he says, quoting Henry James, "is 'another deal of the social pack.' " He adds about James that he finds his vocabulary interesting—his use of the word "compunction" for instance—but "otherwise, I do not get on well with him."

"What is history, what is civilization, what is disaster? Those are the important questions," he insists. In his picturing of the "psychic damage of historical upheaval," I notice that he does not bring along with him a soothing, vainglorious nostalgia. "I feel no nostalgia for the miserable security of the old ways. That is not my point." And then he remembers a line of Koestler's, "Men can add to their knowledge but they cannot subtract." "In my own mind," Naipaul continues, "I change that to: Men cannot unlearn what they have learned."

He tells of traveling in the Congo in 1965 and 1968. "I saw there a rich town, abandoned by the Belgians. Street lamps rusty, sand everywhere, collapsed verandas. The Africans were camping in the houses, just the way the ancient English camped in the abandoned villas of the Romans. Here again in Africa one was back in the 5th century. Native people camping in the ruins of civilization. You could see the bush creeping back

as you stood there . . . When you have watched the bush returning, you
are different from a young man from Harvard or London who is traveling,
doing his project."

Indeed, the bush is everywhere, creeping back, entangling, choking all
those places "going forward." In downtown Trinidad, as well as in
Africa. And what is the bush in Trinidad? "It is the breakdown of
institutions, of the contract between man and man. It is theft, corruption,
racist incitement." In Trinidad, many years before, I had noticed the
sulky separation of the Indians and blacks. "The Indians are one-third of
the population, what is called a large minority. They have no say about
anything, of course," Naipaul said.

In 1972, he went to Argentina. "I was appalled. The people thought
their problems were political, but I see it as the nature of the country, the
way the society was founded. They cannot face things, such as the killing
of the Indians for their land. They lie to themselves every day and try to
invent a sort of cosmic mythology . . . . There is a certain 'scum' quality
in Latin America. They imagine that if you kill the right people every
thing will work. Genocide is their history."

Borges? "His real work is in the poems, not in tales. The poems
celebrate the glorious land and the part played in it by his ancestors. But
it is an awful history, not glorious. It is a bogus past."

The fastidiousness of a Naipaul text, its pride and imaginative careful-
ness, are part of the man himself. Again and again he speaks of "clarity"
and "clear-sightedness": qualities of mind and qualities of style. "For
works to last, they must have a certain clear-sightedness. And to achieve
that, one perhaps needs a few prejudices." In the writing of English, in
the grating of people from different cultures coming together, he says that
he has no models. Most of English fiction today he dismisses as "fairy
tales." Fairy tales. I suppose he means of adultery, family life, social
strain.

In American fiction, "the machinery gets bigger, the layers thinner."
There is not enough questioning of the significant stupidities of society.
"I do not mean poverty and the gross visible injustices. Something
deeper than that, hidden."

In *A Bend in the River* there is a new President a native, somewhere in
French Africa. Perhaps it is Zaire about which he has written before. The
Yvettes and Reymonds, the Indars and Mettys, wake up one morning to
find all swept away. And, Naipaul says, throughout the third word, "The
West is packing its boxes, waiting for the helicopters." This, as I see it,
is his great theme: cultures rising up and going to seed, celebrating and
mourning, all at the same moment.

We return for a moment to questions of style. Freshness of words, he repeats, the freshness of certain 17th-century English prose writers, of the Shakespeare of "Antony and Cleopatra," of "Henry V" the freshness of vision in Balzac's "Lost Illusions": "Balzac told the French where they were."

Someday, he says, he would like to write a narrative fiction something like Gogol's "The Inspector General." "A work of perfect clarity."

"Chekhov? No. Somehow I have lost my admiration for him. To the English middle class, the boredom of the plays is thought to be something aristocratic. But it is only the idleness and helplessness of the trapped. The terrible limitations of society that can, among other things, turn people into chatterboxes."

A few months ago I took a trip to India—that place where Naipaul's intensity of feeling and observation and his historical despair united as in some doomed marriage arranged by the family. Speaking of India he said, "How tired I am of the India-lovers, those who go on about 'beautiful India' the last gasp of hideous, imperialistic vanity. And the mark of a second-rate mind."

When I asked for a deeper explanation of "untouchability" than the journey had provided, he said, "You cannot understand it. No, they cannot rise, cannot 'pass' by way of a meritocracy. It is a question of families, villages, ancestors. No escape. It is slavery, maintained on one meal a day. One meal to be shared by the whole family. You ask why that is? Well, for one thing, if you feed people they will bite you. One-fourth of the population—contaminated. Living in an unending contamination."

Do the well-to-do Indians feel guilt? "Terror, I should think. No guilt."

The millions of women in India, wearing colored dots in the middle of the forehead. I could understand that some distinction was being made if the dots were uncommon, like a large expensive ring. What does the dot actually mean?

"The dot means: My head is empty."

In Naipaul's fiction the narrator is often a lonely, displaced Indian, far from home. Nothing is quite real to him, and yet he must summon a sort of hope, take on enterprises if he can find them. The journey he has taken to London or to Africa, wherever, will turn out to be a comedy, a comedy of a sad and instructive kind. The meager elements of stability the wanderer was seeking—a little store, a bed in a closet in a Washington D.C. apartment—will, so to speak, be "taken over."

At the beginning and end of *In a Free State*, Naipaul speaks in his own voice as a traveler. Many, many travelers, many empires have passed over the old sites. At Luxor, he looks at the Colossus "on whose shin the

Emperor Hadrian had caused to be carved verses in praise to himself, to commemorate his visit.'' In Cairo, the defeated soldiers of the 1967 war, ''trying to walk back home, casting long shadows on the sand.'' It is always the old world, sweating in its heavy woolen modern uniforms.

The sweep of Naipaul's imagination, the brilliant fictional frame that expresses it, are in my view without equal today. Historical ambiguity shades and at the same time brightens, for us at least, these continents and subcontinents, these emerging and sinking worlds he travels in and out of to produce his great life work.

Thinking of the Africa in *A Bend in the River*, I ask: What is the future, in Africa?

His answer: ''Africa has no future.''

Man in a Glass Box

Linda Blandford / 1979

From *Saturday Telegraph Sunday Magazine*, London. 23 September 1979, 77, 81, 86, 90. Reprinted by permission of Ewan MacNaughton Associates©.

In a four-bedroomed, centrally-heated, double-garaged, elegantly-landscaped contemporary ranch house in Connecticut a small dinner party is in progress. Flood-lighting picks up the snowy woods outside. The cheddar cheese, imported from Jermyn Street, has gone round the table and the host, V. S. Naipaul, is extolling the work of the painter whose home he has rented for the year. She is a cloud buff.

"She's devoted her life to these clouds," he announces with a note of languid pity. "So much effort, so much work has gone into these pictures. To what avail? Updike writes golden sentences—and so what? My best sentences are the simple sentences."

A long-legged, well-preserved house guest from New York, oozing desire to please, recalls meeting John Updike, author of *Couples,* at a symposium. "Oh, the shocking mask of narcissism over his face." As the cheese goes round again, this house guest looks over the clouds. "I suppose that's a sincere picture," she offers, "but I don't find it *intimate.*"

Naipaul considers intimacy, while inhaling Fribourg and Treyer snuff through what appears to be an insatiable nostril. The company waits on him; as usual. "Such great talent, such great talent," he sighs. "She spends her time teaching at the university." This last word escapes with distaste.

Naipaul is spending a year teaching creative reading and writing at Wesleyan University, a pretty, well-endowed liberal arts' college. "I would take poison rather than do this for a living. I've always thought of universities in a grand way, as seats of learning and inquiry. Well, it's bogus. You get bogus students taking bogus courses in bogus writing. I thought I'd meet lots of people who passionately wanted to write. I was shocked to find some take the course in the same way as basketwork or karate. I was further shocked to find they thought it was an easy way to get an A grade."

His students were asked to submit anonymous reports, judgments rather, on *his* performance. "He was simply the worst, most close-minded, inconsiderate, uninteresting and incompetent professor I have ever met," reads one that he hugs to himself, almost basking in this newest humiliation.

Naipaul is 46. He has been called by many, including critic and writer Francis Wyndham, "the foremost living novelist writing in English." His books, which include *An Area of Darkness* and *A House for Mr. Biswas,* have been widely acknowledged. *In a Free State* won the 1971 Booker Prize.

Even so, for his latest novel he received an American advance of only 25,000 dollars—a sum normally associated here with a competent biography or promising second novel. He is not unaware of that.

"You know, my work doesn't really exist. When people talk about trends, I'm never there. There is some element of discussion about others of one's contemporaries—Updike, Bellow, Lessing, Amis—but my work will not be around, They won't give *me* a Nobel prize. There'll be nothing in it for Them; I don't represent anything. One doesn't speak for anyone. This is not a complaint, you know. One is just stating a fact."

His voice is beautiful, dark, modulated in the Oxford way. He talks of his work with reverence. "Ever since I can remember, writing to me was a noble calling, a vocation." This might explain his harping on slights and pinpricks, as if they somehow insult that calling. He is quick, for example, to display the latest communication from his American agent tactlessly addressed to N. S. Naipaul.

He has emerged from the latest of his "great labours" (writing *A Bend in the River*) exhausted, quivering with discontent. The book is about a man's struggle for self-sufficiency in Africa, a country where he is a stranger.

What should be a pleasant evening in this rich, pastoral American setting is made uncomfortable by his tension. Only the unmitigated admiration of the house guest from New York seems to soothe him.

She works for PEN, a world association of writers, and is here to arrange a symposium for him in New York. "I want to present you to your literary public. There is a steel rod that goes through your work, Vidia, and what I would like to talk about now is the definition of that rod."

He has reservations. He has already turned down an invitation to read his work at the distinguished Poetry Centre: "I didn't like the man's signature." The contradiction is clear: The longing for recognition, the horror of seeking it. "One wants to do nothing that violates oneself," he explains, shrinking his firm, angular frame into the chair.

The New Yorker wonders at this. Where the power of thought is his

coin, hers is the emotion. She translates this recoil from the glittering
soirée as "your ambivalence about wanting to be loved, Vidia." This
phrase seems to stump him. He repeats it as if trying to understand it by
its sound. "What do you mean, 'wanting to be loved'? This wish, is it
important to you?"

"Oh, I was talking of little violations," explains the New Yorker. "I
have noticed that your work is riddled with the hyper-sensitivity of self-
disgust." At this point Naipaul jumps up, clutches his head and rushes
upstairs. "Another headache," purrs an older friend, who has been
ignored by him all evening.

It is nine o'clock in the morning. A biting wind blows across a land
that is icy hard. Vidia is going horse-riding. The crotchety mood of the
dinner party is still upon him. Once again, he could not sleep.

He does not worry about death ("that holds no fear for me"); he
worries about growing infirm. He fears not having the sheer physical
energy left for many more of his "great labours." He passes too many
nights in a haze of Mandrax and Valium. "On a good night now I sleep
about five hours.

"A lot of the energy I had when I was young came from the ability I
had to sleep eight or nine hours at a time. Insomnia wrecks about half my
working week now. I used to do my best work in the mornings, now, with
this sleeping nonsense, the best part of my work is written through
headaches at six-thirty or seven in the evening. I do think the books are
written in blood."

It is as if he must will himself to survive; probably he has always had
to do so. It is somehow impossible to reconcile this careful, formal man
fussing over wines, cheese, old furniture—all the patina of breeding and
background—with the child he must have been, poor in a colonial
country, the outsider in a white and black West Indies. He is a totally
self-made man; virtually an act of will.

There have been moments when it almost fell apart, this creation of
his. In Oxford, for instance: "The great humiliation of my undergraduate
days had to do with borrowing money and the shame of it." If he was
wretched, he will not, or cannot, talk about it—for that means talking
about his breakdown. "When I was 19 I was very, very ill. All my life
since I recovered has been a great celebration of sanity, of knowing how
a hair's breadth separates one from mental torment. It's too close."

It explains in part the tension that he generates, the mind's implacable
struggle to control his being and all who surround that being. The horse-
riding is part of it. He does it because it's good for him, in the way he
takes draughts of landscape and travel "as antidotes to the cerebral," as

he puts it. He certainly conveys no sense of physical freedom or delight in movement for its own sake ("Dance? I've never danced. I'd be ashamed of it. It is something out of the jungle. It's undignified. I dislike all those lower class cultural manifestations.")

There is no-one else around when he arrives at Bar-H Farm. He tried to ride ten years ago, but so lost his nerve that he could not even mount. Now he shows an almost magnificent contempt for the 15·3 hands horse he leads out to saddle. He scurries to and fro behind its back legs, as if daring it to lash out, despising its subservience. Not for him the appeasing pat or words of reassurance. "Look at this horse," he says afterwards. "It's been running around obeying silly instructions in a purely physical way. At one stage there's affection for the horse. But later, when you realise it's a purely physical object, comes a complete disregard."

It is as if there is no natural affection in him for any creature, only this touching isolation, the loneliness that moves. Once mounted there is both clumsiness and correctness. It's easy to see why he has been described as having "a difficult beauty"—a description which he savours and recalls.

He is none too pleased to find that Joanna will be teaching him today. "She's very tough," he confides, "and I don't like being yelled at." In the ring, he is a picture of pinched suffering.

"Don't worry about the dog," yells Joanna.

"Don't worry about the dog," he repeats grimly.

"Sit back, Videeeo," shouts Joanna. "Come on talk to him, talk to him, for heaven's sake." He remains mute.

"Your reins are uneven, Videeeo; every day we have the *same* thing."

"Same problem," he repeats with disgust.

He is surprisingly good and awesomely determined. "Another triumph of will," he says matter-of-factly as he gets down, insisting that he has enjoyed himself. His trials are not yet over. Joanna bears down on him with buxom humour.

"Hey, Videeeo, you wrote a book?"

"Yes, why?"

"What book?"

"A story."

"Was it published?"

"Yes, yes. YES."

"So what's the name of it?"

"Let's see. Well, *Guerrillas*."

"What's it about?"

"Nasty, wicked people," he says with relish. For the first time today he smiles.

A woman friend describes Naipaul as "a man in a glass box looking out, perceiving everything." He himself talks of an aridity in his life. He has had no children ("They're a waste of time. I grew up in an extended family and I couldn't stand the sight of another pregnant woman.") The father for whom he felt such great affection died when he was 21. ("That's been enough for me in some way.")

He talks of "densing up" with age, through experience, but also through disappointments. The extraordinary comic gift of his youth has been silent for some years. A cold, bleak pessimism runs through his latest works. "I began to feel, when I re-read Tolstoy about ten years ago," he says at one point, "that all great, lasting writers have their vulgarities; some little human impulse which in great writers tends to get magnified. It would be very hard for me to go out and do a 'warm, loving thing'. Probably it shrieks out—my wish to run away from any entanglements. This in the end cuts oneself off from other people. But there you are, to an extent one has slightly created oneself by now."

He is in a dark, dark time here in Connecticut. Perhaps even he does not realise how he attacks everything and everyone, denigrating all, including himself (India? "The country where the disaster has occurred." Blacks? "I'm bored with the black situation. It is of no importance.")

It is hard to remember that this peevish man, wizened by insomnia, all passion spent in the novel, indeed has greatness. He hoards himself; his best and deepest nature is revealed only in that most solitary of occupations, writing. And what might in lesser men seem appalling self-centredness and cruelty is somehow thereby made acceptable.

And were he always this way, he could not have gathered round him those loyal friends who have endured his many bad times—both financial and emotional. They speak of charm, curiosity, enthusiasm ("Joy?" Naipaul shakes his head. "Oh no, I'm never taken out of myself. But pleasure, yes. I would say one's days are full of pleasures.") Old friends talk of dining off a tin of salmon in poorer days with Naipaul, but with the host always graciously at ease: of encounters at Indian art exhibitions, with Naipaul offering himself as a generous and fascinating guide.

Certainly he has held the friendship and devotion of the silvery and gentle woman who waits for him in London. Pat Naipaul married Vidia in 1955. There has not been much in the way of conventional security: no children, no home (he sold the house they eventually bought in Stockwell to finance his travels). In 1966 she gave up the teaching job of which he disapproved ("She worked so hard and I don't think any child is worth that effort.'') In the enclosed world of their marriage, Vidia has always taken centre stage; she always placed in the shadows, working hard to support him. She may have known loneliness and sacrifice, but never boredom.

Since Vidia decided not to take her with him to America, she has been able to spend the year quietly in England. It has been a time of small pleasures and indulgences. In the corner of their tiny two-roomed flat in Kensington there is a pile of old newspapers. Before he comes home she will throw them out (''hiding the evidence of my crimes,'' she says wryly). Vidia hates mess.

The flat is like a perfect dolls' house: peaceful, fastidiously neat. There are green walls, slub curtains, a few choice pieces of old furniture. The books suggest the scholar; his own are discreetly out of the way. There are no reviews casually left around, no photographs of the author with great personages. Naipaul does not need to impress his personality on his surroundings in that way. Only the pictures suggest his influence and recall his Brahmin origins: Jageanor in the mounts of Srinagar, Rampugur, near Benares, on the River Ganges.

Pat Naipaul is distressed to hear that in America her husband seems so discontented. It is obviously not a new story. ''Oh Vidia exaggerates everything,'' she says with a mixture of concern, pride and exasperation. ''I'll tell you the important thing about him: he believes it has to be agony to write. In fact it is Vidia's supreme joy.''

While his wife waits for the moment when she can go to the hairdresser and buy flowers to celebrate his return, Vidia Naipaul, with the air of a martyred hero, is finishing his course at Wesleyan. On the door to his lecture room in Wilbur Fisk Hall, a notice reads: ''The sexual assault class has been cancelled.'' This is America.

Forbiddingly dressed in black, with dark glasses, Naipaul enters and buries himself in Balzac, seemingly unaware that at least five of his 15 creative reading students have neglected to provide themselves with books. If he senses their silent hostility, he dismisses it. But for those who are prepared to go out to him, to seek what he has to offer, it is a privileged experience. This, after all, is a master of words exploring that which matters most to him—the art of literature.

Afterwards, in his bare college room, into which he has conspicuously not moved one book, file or piece of paper, he reflects on V. S. Naipaul, nearing 50. ''You can't imagine at 25 what it is like to be a writer at 45. The practice of the profession has altered one. One has been slightly broken and damaged by one's disappointments. But very recently I have begun to feel confident of my talent. I feel I have extended it and, because of that, it has possessed me in a way it didn't quite when I was young.

"I've stretched myself. Right from the start I've gone on doing difficult things, not out of perversity but out of experience. And because I've taken it to the limit of my talent, I've come to know myself. It has completely taken me over. I am nothing but my vocation really."

How many books, he questions, does he still have in him? "I hope that when I cease to have anything to say I'll stop. But if I stop thinking, if I stop feeling, if I'm not compelled to do something with those impressions, those thoughts, I don't think life will have meaning."

A softer, more vulnerable person looks out of those large, brown eyes. Now it is possible to see why so many admire, and some love, this awkward man. "You know, I feel I'm a bad advertisement for my work. That is one reason why I'm slightly ashamed of meeting people who've read it. I feel I might let the work down." Perhaps he means it. Either way, he has never seemed so likeable, or so wrong.

Life, Literature, and Politics: An Interview with V. S. Naipaul

Cathleen Medwick / 1981

From *Vogue,* August 1981, 129–30. Courtesy *Vogue*© 1981, reprinted by permission of The Condé Nast Publications Inc.

It is difficult for Americans to imagine what it would be like to be on their own—stripped of America, with its vast pride, its territorial imperatives, its unrelenting sense of history. An American writer, even an expatriate, is always aware of (and often haunted by) his country's potency. The same is, of course, true for a Russian, an Englishman, a German. For each, the land of his birth is, in the most basic sense, a "fatherland": the expatriate may despise his country, but he can never ignore it.

V. S. Naipaul, on the other hand, is a man without a country. Born in Trinidad, he went to England at the age of eighteen: there, "untrammeled by the accidents of history or background," he hoped to have a romantic career as a writer. The romance proved illusory, but he did write. Returning to his island years later, Naipaul discovered that there was nothing to come home to. Trinidad was, for him, a collapsed, indifferent society with no respect for its past, and no regard for its future. Since that discovery, Naipaul has traveled and explored other cultures—India, Argentina, Africa, Asia—seeking, in their failures, some explanation of his own loss.

He travels secretly, quietly, an almost invisible observer. His own identity remains, in spite of the critical acclaim for his books, a mystery. Talking with Naipaul, on the rare occasions when he stays somewhere long enough to talk, is a process of ready signs, gestures. You have the sense of being in the company of a man who has discovered (among other things) the most graceful way out.

He is small, composed, and—once you look closely at his face, his sensuous mouth and weary, critical eyes—a worldly-looking man. Something of a dandy, too, a lover of fine wines and seasonings and snuff. Sitting he is a paragon of stillness, watching everyone in the politest way—eyebrows lifted, pleasantly entertained.

We are having tea at New York's Algonquin Hotel. Assenting to a piece of cake, Naipaul eats it briskly, without fuss. But when someone remarks on his appetite, be becomes attentive—not fearful, but intensely curious: "Is it too much? Am I eating too much?"

Later, leaving the restaurant, he rushes ahead of us. We see him threading through the complicated lobby, then off in a blur, the way a camera streaks through intervening footage from one scene to the next. The blur is deceptive: Naipaul knows exactly where he is.

We are at dinner, at the apartment of people who know his work. He is voluble, boyish among his admirers ("I have a talent for relaxing people," he says). He savors details ("That chair, do you think it is hand turned? Lovely!"), bringing the objects forward, one by one. That is how he brings people out: with a director's particularity.

Just after dessert—we are still at the table—Naipaul decides that it is time to leave. He is at the door in a minute. In the cab to the hotel where he is staying, and where we are going to talk, Naipaul turns to me: "It is very important," he says, in a much quieter voice than he has used all evening, "to know how to cut things off."

The art of departure. After Naipaul left Trinidad ("a dot on the map of the world," he has called it, "a place with no history") he turned to India, the ancestral homeland from which his grandfather had emigrated as an indentured laborer. But India turned out to be a myth, an "area of darkness" with no afterglow from its past. India had survived poorly. It was, in Naipaul's view, "one step from the roses of Kashmir to a potful of plastic daisies."

It had been hard to leave Trinidad; harder to renounce India, because that had always been his reference point, the indicator of where he belonged. When he talks about India, Naipaul's face begins to curve downward: it tends that way, like a mask. Then, the sadness articulates itself, becomes an instrument of judgment:

"India has been a shock for me because—you know, you think of India as a very old and civilized land, it is the land of your ancestors. One took this idea of an antique civilization for granted and thought that it contained the seed of growth in this century, in this new civilization. And I've seen it probably doesn't . . . the triviality of Indian thought. The poverty of its leadership . . . India has nothing to contribute to the world, is contributing nothing to the world at the moment."

The harsh verdict, clearly rendered, is Naipaul's way of exorcising a myth.

The way civilizations delude themselves, the way they make cocoons out of their cultural myths, and die inside them, is Naipaul's great theme. His work, both fiction and non-fiction, is a crisscrossing of odysseys made by people who want to "attach themselves . . . to other civilizations, with other drives," because their own have failed them. But these people only succeed in becoming aliens, with no sense of who they are or why they have come.

In the opening essay of *The Return of Eva Perón,* Naipaul writes about a man called Malik, but also known as Michael X—a Trinidadian con-man who went to England to become a Black Power leader or, rather, to promote the illusion of his own leadership: "He was shallow and unoriginal; but he sensed that in England, provincial, rich and very secure, race was, to Right and Left, a topic of entertainment. And he became an entertainer." Malik's journey, and his transformation through contact with "civilized" society, is the kind of movement that fascinates Naipaul. He is always writing about it. In the essay "The Return of Eva Perón" he tracks the Eva Perón legend: how it grew in an Argentina that, by clinging to its colonial myth, lost sight of its impoverished reality. Eva Perón destroyed that myth, and replaced it with her own image. The dead, embalmed, miraculously undecayed Eva Perón becomes the image of Argentina, "magical, debilitating," petrified by its own dreams.

Naipaul's judgments on flawed civilizations are as accurate as they are, often, ruthless. Unlike other writers, buttressed by an easy patriotism, Naipaul feels no compulsion to be charitable. It is the attitude of someone who has nothing more to lose.

"A dark vision," as Irving Howe has said. Most critics agree—and here is where some negative criticism has surfaced alongside the praise—that there is in Naipaul's work a pervading pessimism, which may be his flaw. Howe speculates that the work's dark vision may reveal some insufficiency, or lack of resolution, in the man himself.

Q: *"Do you think that writers reveal themselves in their work?"*

A: "The writer sets out to do certain things. The writer doesn't always know what he has done. He doesn't really know himself; because that's the point about being a writer. There's always something more that you've set out to do. And I suppose, with some, there's always something less. People give themselves away completely in their fiction."

Q: *"Do you give yourself away?"*

A: "I must do, I must."

What about the "dark vision" in his work?

"But if the vision were really dark then it would be very hard to put pen to paper. One would be so . . . distressed. There'd be no point, the experience has gone beyond writing. You've got to compose yourself to write, after all. You need peace, you need calm. You need a publisher, you need critics, booksellers, you need all the apparatus of order. If you rejected that, you couldn't write."

The "apparatus of order" is what Naipaul has equipped himself with

in his travels about the world. It is what gives him his sense of direction.
That apparatus includes the house where he works ("I live in a very
special sort of way in England") in the countryside near Salisbury—a
peaceful place. His relationships, he says, are in order too ("My sentimental life has been very simple"—he has been married since 1955, has
no children). And there is an order to Naipaul's way of traveling ("something I learned, a skill"), nothing restless or chaotic about it.

"What's happened, with all the work I've done, is that I've been quite
secure. It's because I understand it all, the way the world is made. I don't
go around thinking about where do I start . . . you can't go around being
too dramatic about being rootless, you know."

Readers have tried to identify Naipaul as a romantic wanderer, an
exile. But he rejects that image. His manner is businesslike; and his
business is to know where he is.

Q: *"Isaac Singer has said that every writer must have roots, must
write out of a strong sense of where he comes from . . ."*

A: "But surely the two things you've said to me are different. Every
writer must write out of a strong sense of where he comes from. But that
doesn't mean necessarily having roots. I think to have roots might cause
one to become a kind of parochial writer. You know, you're writing about
the morals, the manners, of a particular group. Whereas I feel the themes
are other today. The themes might be quite opposite . . . In a very brutal
way, one knows exactly where one's come from, one knows why one
has come."

Has his work taken a particular direction since the early books?

"Yes, the discovery of the way the world is organized. You see, I began
at a time when the world was beginning to change. Empires were
withdrawing, and I had a kind of childish faith that there was going to be
a reorganization of the world. That it was going to be all right. The
discovery has been that it isn't going to be all right. The discovery has
been, you know, you have to come face to face with a very simple
question: why is it that certain countries and certain peoples have allowed
themselves to be exploited and abused? What is it in them that permits
this? What is their flaw? And you find that perhaps their flaws are still
with them, that the flaws aren't always external, in other people's
hostility. Flaws might be within, in the limitations of particular peoples,
the limitations of their civilization or their culture."

How does he feel about America, now that he's been here some
months?

"I know so little of America . . . But success tends to breed, as in
England . . . ."

A complacency?

"Yes, and a misconception of the things that led to that success. People think it has to do with the water. It has to do with the rain. It has to do with the land. It has to do with the race. They forget it probably has to do with brutal things like intelligence and endeavor and enterprise. They regard it as a kind of magic particular to a particular part of the earth, a blessing on a particular people. They don't see that it has in fact been created, that success comes after endeavor and effort. And people tend to hold onto or imitate what is easily imitable. Manners. Particular clothes. The tweeds, the accents. As though these things then become achievements. You hold onto the symbols of your country and your culture, and it's not enough."

A method of observation: "Direct looking," Naipaul has called it, the stripping of things to their bare surface. It is a violent response (the violence surprises him) but also a kind of detachment—that of a physician who dissects a body to take a look at the disease. It is also the detachment of the Hindu mystic—and that is an ironic legacy.

So there is a corollary to Naipaul's "dark vision": the way he has learned to utilize it as an instrument of order.

"But when I am writing, I always feel that to come to some comprehension or acceptance of what is true is itself a kind of liberation. Then I thought that perhaps that wasn't enough. Because when we read fiction we're like children to some extent. The strong instinct is for everyone to live happily ever afterwards. So then I thought, in addition to the truth, there was a way to combat the dissatisfaction the reader will feel at something that appears to end without solace for men."

He is very still, waiting for the question.

"And what is that?"

"Comedy. I thought, *that* is it. That all one could offer is comedy, real comedy."

Up to now, there has been little "real comedy" in Naipaul's work. Biting satire there is, presented by characters whose sense of humor is stronger than their hopes.

"Probably, the comedy has been suppressed because one has been working toward the discovery of one's themes, you know. The discovery of themes is after all the major work of any writer—themes that are particular to him.

"You know the phrase we use about curling up with a book. I would like to work back toward that."

A Bend in the River—precise, relentless in its clarity of vision—is a difficult book, not one to curl up with. The prose runs along with a deceptive smoothness. Events, like stones thrown into a clear pool, have ramifications. As always, Naipaul is writing about journeys, about people who make them and where they lead. He is writing about beginnings, and new beginnings. He makes great circles: always widening, and at the center there is always a point of stillness—another Hindu motif. So the sense of direction is itself, in a way, a delusion. The narrator of *A Bend in the River* reports, of his journey into Africa: "Each day's drive was like an achievement; each day's achievement made it harder for me to turn back." At the same time, the narrator is saying to himself: "But this is madness. I am going in the wrong direction. There can't be a new life at the end of this." Journeys do not always mean progress, and all that one can really know is the right moment to leave.

The art of departure: it is Naipaul's way of shaking off the past.

Q: *"Was it your traveling that taught you how to leave, 'how to cut things off?' "*

A: "No, that comes from social incompetence in one's youth, and not knowing when to leave, when to tell people it was over."

Q: *"Does that apply to closer relationships too?"*

A: "To all relations, every encounter. There's always a time to call them off. And you call them off."

At a certain point in *A Bend in the River,* the narrator ends his love affair with another man's wife. It is a violent end—violence done to the woman—which some readers (especially women) have had trouble accepting.

Q: *"At dinner, you talked about love, writing about love, and about the sexual act . . . ."*

A: "The nature of it, yes, and not writing in the standard way . . . . My experience is that very few women have experienced true passion. And they probably—you know my feelings? My feeling is that most people are terribly inept in sex and passion."

Q: *"Men and women?"*

A: "I think it is a failing of men, yes, because everything starts with the man."

Naipaul is beginning, again, to answer his own questions.

"No. passion is a very lovely thing. It's worth everything. I think it's worth everything."

It is almost midnight. Tomorrow morning Naipaul will return to England. Again, he is about to disappear from view. But, at least for now, he shows no sign of wanting to leave.

Q: *"What will you do now that you're going back to England? Do you know if you'll begin writing again soon?"*

A: "I'll be going on a journey fairly soon. I'm going to certain countries, but I'd rather not say where. I'm going on a journey."

The Dark Visions of V. S. Naipaul

Charles Michener / 1981

From *Newsweek*, 16 November 1981, 104–105, 108–110, 112, 114–115. Reprinted by permission of Newsweek Inc.©

For sheer abundance of talent there can hardly be a writer alive who surpasses V. S. Naipaul . . . . Naipaul struggles with the ordeals and absurdities of living in new "third world" countries. He is free of any romantic moonshine about the moral charms of primitives or the glories of flood-stained dictators. Nor does he show a trace of Western conde- scension or nostalgia for colonialism.
> —Irving Howe, reviewing *A Bend in the River*,
> *The New York Times Book Review*, 1979

Naipaul the writer now flows directly into Naipaul the social phenome- non, the celebrated sensibility on tour . . . [He] carries with him a kind of half-stated but finally unexamined reverence for the colonial order. [There is] a deep emptiness in Naipaul the writer for which Naipaul the social phenomenon is making others pay . . . All this to promote an attitude of distant concern and moral superiority in the reader.
> —Edward Said, reviewing "Among the Believers,"
> *New Statesman*, 1981

V. S. Naipaul was born in Trinidad in 1932. He came to England in 1950 to do a university course, and began to write, in London, in 1954. He has followed no other profession.
> —Author's note in the Penguin editions of the
> books of V.S. Naipaul

He appears, at first glance, an unlikely lightning rod for such praise, such denunciation. Compactly built, carefully dressed in a herringbone-tweed jacket, gray flannels, a light-colored knit tie against a surprising burgundy-colored shirt, he sits behind black-rimmed glasses in the London hotel lobby—an Indian professor of Vedic literature, perhaps, comfortably absorbed into England's multiracial woodwork, waiting to be met for lunch.

Just 49, Naipaul has published an astonishing seventeen books, won every major literary prize in Britain and is a perennial favorite for the Nobel Prize. His latest work of nonfiction, *Among the Believers: An*

Islamic Journey (430 pages. Knopf. $15.), has just appeared. The fruit of six months of travel through four countries gripped by Islamic fundamentalism, it is a brilliant report of social illness that will be instantly familiar to Naipaul readers: sharp-eyed wanderings through the frenzy of Teheran traffic, the shrine-filled province of Sind, the Intercontinental lobbies of Kuala Lumpur, the postcard villages of Java, encounters with a few people of power and with many more of no power, uncompromising pronouncements of "great flaws" in what he has called the "half-made" societies of the world: "This late-twentieth-century Islam . . . offered only the Prophet, who would settle everything—but who had ceased to exist. This political Islam was rage, anarchy." The journey seems to have cost the traveler some pain. "I'm not in fighting shape," he says. "Nothing wrong. Just tired. Stop me if I start to have more than one glass of wine."

What happened to *him* during those travels through Islam? "I began to understand a good deal more man's capacity for lying and self-deception," he says. "I began to feel the tragedy of people who are really so ill-equipped for the twentieth century, who are light years away from making the tools they've grown to like."

But isn't the West partly to blame for the Islamic turmoil? "I'm not interested in attributing *fault*," he says sharply. "I'm interested in civilizations. If Arabs piss on my doorstep in South Kensington, I can't *not* notice. It's silly to pretend they're *not* barbarians." Well, aren't there a few barbarians in the West, too? "England is the least-educated country in Europe. It isn't only Africans who are bow-and-arrow people, it's so many people here, living at a very high material level, who have allowed their minds to go slack. The English bourgeoisie are mimicking their former roles. They express their soul by the color of their walls. They put dreadful pictures on their walls and *stagger* them!" He takes out a little canister of snuff and, with the tip of a key, delicately builds a mound of brown powder on the crook of a thumb and inhales it. "Such a disagreeable habit!" he says. "But I'm a tobacco lunatic. I need it profoundly. They say," he adds with a chuckle, "that the battlefield of Waterloo is littered with snuff canisters."

How has he changed over the years? "Until not too many years ago," he says with deliberateness, "there was a sensual aridity in my life. When I came to England, I had nothing. I had no great personal beauty and charm. I really only had intelligence, along with a good deal of historical and social ignorance. It's one reason why I've had to read great books two or three times as I get older in order to understand them. Until not many years ago, I felt very, very deprived." Does he miss having children? "I never wanted them," he says simply. "I couldn't bear to bring anyone into the world to suffer."

Such candor is more than Naipaul's attractive practice of meeting every question head on. It suggests that, after so many years of "public" novels and essays, he is now wrestling with private matters. What is he reading these days? "Proust—straight through in the new English edition. It has caused me to think a lot, to feel there is a kind of falsity about the usual novel. Proust realized that the nature of society and one's life today are not really amenable to the novel form—one needs something bigger. Reading him up to 'Guermantes Way,' I felt inadequate, that I wasn't up to him. And this may shock you, but I feel that I don't want to be a writer unless I am at the very top. You see, from the age of 16, I've given more than my life to being a writer."

What will he write next? He sighs. "Part of the problem of writing is that you use up your experience. The great triumph is to go on. We do come to these profound ditches. I might be at one now."

Naipaul left Trinidad when he was 17. "When I was in the fourth form I wrote a vow on the endpaper of my 'Kennedy's Revised Latin Primer' to leave within five years. I left after six; and for many years afterwards in England, falling asleep in bedsitters with the electric fire on, I had been awakened by the nightmare that I was back in tropical Trinidad." This urge to get out, so vividly described in *The Middle Passage*, Naipaul's book of travel essays about the West Indies, gives him kinship with the "very top" escape artists of modern literature—Conrad, Joyce, Hemingway.

But there is a crucial difference. Naipaul is twice displaced: in the 1880s his father's father was brought to Trinidad from India. "He carried his village with him," writes Naipaul in *An Area of Darkness*, his account of passage from a childhood sense of India as a "resting-place for the imagination" to the horrifying place itself. Naipaul is, of all the great Western writers of exile, the most rootless, the last fortified by the tradition in which he writes. His birthplace was "a materialist immigrant society, continually growing and changing, never settling into any pattern, always retaining the atmosphere of the camp." Within that society was his Hindu family, so fearful of outside "contamination" that, when he left, he had eaten in restaurants only three times.

But there was an example to be built upon—his father, Seepersad Naipaul, a rebellious Brahmin, avid reader of Dickens, journalist for the *Trinidad Guardian*. In 1943 he published at his own expense a small collection of short stories about Indian life in Trinidad, which became a local best seller. Six years later his older son, Vidiadhar Surajprasad, won a Trinidad government scholarship to study at Oxford.

"My father had a prodigious sense of irony, a way of turning all disaster into comedy, which he transmitted to his children. [Besides a younger brother, Shiva, who also writes, Naipaul has five sisters.] I always felt an immense tenderness towards him. His death, when I was 21, remains one of the biggest events of my life."

Did he die happy? "No, he was unhappy much of the time. But he had a tremendous gift for joy which I share. Happiness is a kind of passive animal state, isn't it? Whereas joy is a positive sensation of delight in a particular thing—a joke, another person, a meal—and you can have it in the middle of deep gloom. The side of my character that keeps me going came from my mother, I suppose. My mother is really a perfect Asiatic. I don't think she has ever experienced emotions that are particular to *her*; all of her pleasures and pains are experienced as ritual moments. In his modest way, my father was in revolt against all this.

"I have two very early childhood memories: of my father being mentally ill for some time and of my waking up in a hospital room and being strapped in bed. Pneumonia, my mother tells me. But I have always been fighting a hysteria that plagued me as a child." What activates it? "The old fear of extinction, and I mean of dying. I mean the fear of being reduced to nothing, of feeling crushed. It's partly the old colonial anxiety of having one's individuality destroyed. And it also goes back to the family I grew up in—a typically Indian extended family. The thing you must understand about that sort of family is that it's a microcosm of the authoritarian state, where power is all-important. I withdrew. By the age of 14, I think I knew almost everything about human behavior from having grown up in that kind of family—at least the worst things." Did he know the best, too? "No, that had to be acquired later. It was one of the things I journeyed to England for."

How has he coped with his hysteria? "I'll tell you a story. I had my own breakdown. It came oddly enough when I was at Oxford and I was watching a film which I was loving—*The African Queen*. And just when Bogart said something to Katharine Hepburn about sleeping one off or something, I could take it no longer and left the cinema. What form did it take? One was terrified of human beings. One didn't wish to show oneself to them. I did see a doctor about it. Everything he said was absolutely right. I hated him for saying it and stopped seeing him. I cured myself. It took me two years. Intellect and will, intellect and will. And the only thing that gave me solace, which didn't create pictures of human beings,

was the intricacy of language. I lost myself in my studies of the deriva-
tions of words, the design of the lettering."

Naipaul left Oxford in 1954 and got work at the BBC, editing a literary
program called "Caribbean Voices." At 16 he had written an unpublishable "funny novel about black people" and now he started another
novel—"intensely tragic"—that was soon abandoned. One day at the
BBC he began a story called "Bogart," about a ne'er-do-well in Trinidad
who models himself on the movie star, and without pausing he wrote the
first story of *Miguel Street*, a collection of seventeen sketches of stunted
Port of Spain dreamers, narrated through the maturing eyes of a boy who
will eventually escape. André Deutsch, the British publishing firm, accepted the stories and two subsequent Naipaul novels, *The Mystic Masseur* and *The Suffrage of Elvira*.

There is a surreal simplicity about these early books, which are satires
set almost entirely in Trinidad's Indian community. The risk with satire
is to sound overworked. Naipaul's great gift, present at the beginning, is
to sound utterly unworked: the characters are exotic, their English
amusingly pidgin, but there is no sense of *quaintness*. And the writer's
poise is formidable. *The Mystic Masseur* is a breath-takingly sustained
black joke: what seems a charming tale of the slippery rise of a harmless
quack becomes the chilling exposé of a complete charlatan (Pundit
Ganesh Ramsumair transformed into "G. Ramsay Muir, M.B.E."). *The
Suffrage of Elvira* is a broader satire about the coming of "democracy"
to Trinidad, which ends as a quietly shattering comedy of community
self-destruct on. In both novels, the feeling of a young man's mockery,
too close to the surface, leaves a slightly bitter aftertaste.

This is absent from *Miguel Street*. In one sketch, about a poet named
B. Wordsworth who has never written a line of poetry, Naipaul achieved
a small masterpiece of comic pathos that foreshadows his great novel *A
House for Mr. Biswas*. The poet tells the boy/narrator that he writes just
one "good line" a month. "What was last month's good line?" asks the
boy. "He looked up at the sky, and said, '*The past is deep.*' I said, 'It is
a beautiful line.' "

At the firm of André Deutsch, which has published all of his books in
England, Naipaul's editor, Diana Athill, says: "He's such a fusspot! If
you change so much as an inverted comma, he'll spot it and change it
back," Once she recalls, the prize catch nearly got away. Hurt by what
he thought was an unsympathetic response at Deutsch to his 1975 novel,
Guerrillas, Naipaul signed on with a new publisher. Then he saw that
publisher's catalog with a blurb hailing him as a "West Indian writer."
He immediately canceled the contract and came back to Deutsch.

"I've been breaking away from that tag all my life," says Naipaul.
" 'West Indian' is a political word. It's all the things I reject. It's not
me." When did he really feel himself a *writer*? "When I was writing
Mystic Masseur, I went to a bookshop and bought Maugham's *The
Painted Veil*, thinking it would teach me about dialogue, and it was
rubbish! And my confidence grew when I began to review books for *The
New Statesman*. Anthony Powell introduced me, and because they were
invariably bad books, one had the lesson of how *not* to write, of what
was shoddy sensibility.

"It took me three years to write *Biswas*, taking time out every fourth
week to support myself writing reviews. The hard thing in writing is
getting to the stage where it begins to *stick*, where the words are *around*
something. It's like taking a whip and trying to wrap it around a rail. I
used to think that I could never be adequately rewarded for what I'd put
into this book, that if someone said they'd give me a million pounds to
stop writing it, I'd say, 'Go away, keep your money'."

A House for Mr. Biswas is Naipaul's most prodigious piece of imaginative writing. The novel, which appeared in 1961, has a "plot" that
nineteenth-century writers would have scrapped: a man, married young,
gets trapped by powerful in-laws, tries to extricate himself by a series of
little rebellions, ekes out a career as a journalist, finally buys his dream
house—a shoddy affair—and dies at the early age of 46. But on this
slender life, which is inspired by his father's, Naipaul has constructed a
marvelous prose epic that matches the best nineteenth-century novels for
richness of comic insight and final, tragic power.

Many of Naipaul's obsessive themes are here: the ill-made hero trying
to find his own place in the world; irrational, morally smug despotism,
embodied by the royal fainting fits of the hero's monstrous mother-in-
law; greed, and the mimicry of a more successful culture. Here are
Naipaul's first descriptions that are both lyrical and appalling—an old
French plantation with the decaying fecundity of Eden, natural disasters,
stupefying slums. And here is the first, full demonstration of Naipaul's
extraordinary, quietly gripping narrative style: simple, active sentences;
simple, vivid vocabulary; a subtle orchestration of comedy, irony and
pathos through the meticulous accumulation of human and natural detail
(Mr. Biswas's slack calves speak paragraphs)—the whole intention being,
as Naipaul once put it, to achieve a novel "indistinguishable from truth."

At the heart of the novel is the only fully developed love story he has
written—that of the father and his brighter son, who will go out to take
on the greater world. If *Biswas* is never heavy, it may be because it is the

last thing Naipaul has written with something of a child's view still in him. For all its darkness, it is his "Kim."

Naipaul suggests a trip to the British Museum. In the entrance hall, he pauses to note with a smile a busy group of Middle Eastern women, their faces veiled. In a favorite gallery of ancient Assyrian art, he stops before a huge frieze labeled "Hunting Wild Onagers and Slaying Lions, 668–627 B.C." "It's fabulous," he says of the grandly violent scene. "Modern art really has very little new to say. Look at the minute detail, the modeling of the humans."

Isn't it interesting that such great art can have so little moral sense, no awareness of cruelty? Naipaul replies: "Ah, but not literary art, which *must* have that sense. Pictures and music can escape it but not an art which deals in words and people."

Some critics charged Naipaul himself with cruelty after he began to travel and produce his wounding, wounded reports on the West Indies and India. West Indian intellectuals attacked him for narrowness and arrogance after *The Middle Passage* appeared in 1962, with its stinging comments about a society so ramshackle as to be indifferent "to virtue as well as to vice." After *An Area of Darkness*, his account of a year in India, appeared in 1964, Indian intellectuals complained about his preoccupation with squalor and filth.

But these are chastening books. *The Middle Passage* is precocious about racial assertion: "Negro racialism . . . has profound intellectual promptings . . . in the realization that the Negro problem lies not simply in the attitude of other to the Negro, but in the Negro's attitude to himself." *An Area of Darkness* flashes with unexpected insights—not least about the author's own Hindu soul. Back in London, "facing my own emptiness," Naipaul writes at the book's end: "I saw how close in the past year I had been to the total Indian negation . . . I felt it as something true which I could never adequately express and never seize again."

"Emptiness" is the specter that haunts Naipaul's two novels of this period. In *Mr. Stone and the Knights Companion* (1963), a gently macabre, all-English dance of death, he sketches an aging, clockwork librarian in a London suburb who makes his one and only bid for success before subsiding into genteel oblivion. In *The Mimic Men*, published four years later, his hero is a 40-year-old Indian from the West Indies, once a rich and idealistic "new man" in Caribbean politics, now disgraced and writing his memoirs in a suburban London hotel. It is one of Naipaul's bleakest works, his first novel about the devastating allure of politics (the hero's mordant dictum is, "Hate oppression: fear the oppressed") and sex ("Intimacy: it was violation and self-violation"). And its hero is very much like the Naipaul who wrote an essay in 1967 called "What's Wrong With Being a Snob?" in which he inveighed against those who romanticize "the oppressed," deny "differences" and write novels that "reduce man to flesh capable only of pleasure or pain." It ended with this cry of dissent: "I do not want to be like them."

Naipaul and his wife of many years, Pat, a slight, bright-eyed Englishwoman of great courtesy whom he met at Oxford, keep a tiny London flat in South Kensington off Gloucester Road. In recent years he has written mostly in a rented cottage in Wiltshire. He is now building a house of his own nearby, and he asks: "Would you like to see it?"

Driving to Wiltshire, he says: "I have to travel. Unless my imagination can be released from all these familiar deadening scenes, I will go stale. My travel is so different from that of Graham Greene and others. They're travelers in a world that's been made safe for them by empire. They write books in which they can imagine the Europeanness of their characters against the native background. The primary difference between my travel and theirs is that while they travel for the picturesque, I'm *desperately* concerned about the countries I'm in." But what is to be done about them? "Nothing! There's nothing to be done. Except we mustn't romanticize them. People must do things for themselves."

He suggests a stop at Winchester. In the vastness of the cathedral, his eye is for the detail—and the spirit behind it. He stops in front of a huge font: "Look at the Norman font! Utterly brutal, utterly brutal, utterly brutal!" Walking past war-memorial plaques under stained-glass windows that commemorate England's dead in imperial battles, he remarks: "A century of war and they put up a window!"

His new house is two old houses put together—brick, tile-roofed, with a Constable view of hills and gullies. Inside, it is snug but airy, very English. "Is it all right? Do you *like* it?" he asks. Does he plan a flower garden? "No," he replies firmly. "I see flowers in other people's gardens all year. I can carry them in my head."

A few minutes away is his rented cottage. The walls are decorated with Naipaul's collection of old Indian miniature paintings. "Bought very cheaply, now worth a lot," he says. He suggests taking one of his two favorite walks—down to a river or up a hill with a view of Stonehenge. "Let's do the river," he decides. His stride in Wellington boots is firm. How does he stay in shape? "I do a lifelong exercise—a yoga for asthma. I stand, go back on my hands and rock. I'm very proud of having a beautiful physique. The body is the one thing we can control. It's a kind of envelope that contains the soul."

And his other private pleasures? "Someone asked me many years ago what I enjoyed best—this was before my sensual life really kindled—and I named three things: I like meeting new people, I take great delight in landscapes, and I like a nicely arranged dinner party where one feels cherished." By what sort of people? "Well, I go out very little. I've become so withdrawn. I think it has to do with my travels. I've been working very hard in the last eight years."

In the cottage, he discusses his new book. Did he read much Islamic literature beforehand? "Not too much. I wanted an open mind. There's an awful lot of missionary stuff being passed off as scholarship by people who lie, who won't call a parasite a parasite, a barbarian a barbarian. Who say, 'Poor little wog, poor little cannibal, he hasn't had his fresh meat today'." Why did he talk to so few political leaders? "They have nothing to tell me. Their views are well known. I try to find out how a society works, what drives the people on."

But isn't what he sees what he wants to see? "*Nothing* was falsified. I'm very, very scrupulous about that. And I have seldom been misled by people because in every new situation I'm always with the other man, I'm always looking at the world through *his* eyes." But, surely, the differences between him and many of the people he meets in those countries are very great. "It's a matter of observing where people are made by false hopes, political beliefs, tribal causes. People with causes inevitably turn themselves off intellectually."

Is there any cause he would support? A long silence. "I am devoted to the idea of the life of the mind. I'm interested in the spread of humane values. I went to a Catholic wedding in Essex about two weeks ago; I was gripped by the experience. It was all new to me, very fresh! I saw the altar, the wine and the wafer. I saw the links with the classical world of bloody sacrifice. And I saw that what had been added by Christianity to the old idea of appeasement of the gods was this endless message of love, of *charity*, man to man. Not that Christianity hasn't done harm, but that Christian idea of love, added to the Roman idea of laws, of contracts, is what has made Western civilization!"

Acts of "love" or "charity"—they are not much in evidence in Naipaul's recent work. In 1969 he published *The Loss of El Dorado*, a brilliant reconstruction of Trinidad's buried colonial history in which he tells the story of advanced civilizations—Spain, France and England— fighting over the meager spoils of a primitive Eden and planting the evil of slavery. It is a tale of mutual corruption—the wilderness has its powers, too—and it focuses on two emblematic episodes: the Europeans' mad search for a city of gold and a British governor's torture of a mulatto girl. Naipaul's subsequent books are set in today's "post-colonial" times, but the story is still the same—except that the difference between what is civilized and what is primitive has blurred; now, the ex-slaves have become as deluded and rapacious as their ex-masters.

In a Free State (1971), *Guerrillas* (1975), *A Bend in the River* (1979)— these novels have established Naipaul's reputation as a modern master. Their titles are deeply ironic. In the first book there is no freedom among the white- and dark-skinned expatriates, only loss of identity. There is no real revolutionary action among the title characters of the second—only pretension and, finally, a murder committed out of sexual shame. There is no promise of building a stable settlement along a nourishing waterway, as implied in the third title. To call Naipaul, as some critics have done, "the scourge of the Third World," "the bearer of bad news from the Other Side," is much too limiting: his sense of breakdown is global, the Other Side is *here*.

In one of the interconnected stories that make up *In a Free State*, an Indian cook, uprooted from Bombay to Washington, D.C., finds himself in a city where blacks are burning and looting and Hare Krishna cultists are dancing in the streets. While Jimmy Ahmed, the Chinese/black leader of a "self-help" commune in the Caribbean, dreams his black-power dreams in *Guerrillas*, the country is being run by American officials of the bauxite company, who fly down from the States, reading pornographic novels on the plane. Salim, the Indian shopkeeper, barely escapes from "the bend in the river" before the town is wiped out in a racial purge by the African dictator, the Big Man. Where will he go except to join the other "lost" Indians who run kiosks and restaurants on London's Gloucester Road? And what will happen to his Indian friends who set up a Bigburger concession in the heart of darkness?

Is Naipaul's vision as critics have charged, too fixed on failure? Is his acerbity that of a dark-skinned man's too-zealous conversion to Western tastes? These questions are really political ones, raised to score political points. Such critics usually overlook one of the most salutary aspects of Naipaul's attitude toward the Third World—Naipaul refuses to condescend or, as he says in his essay on "snobbery," to indulge in a "romanticism [that] begins by sympathizing with the oppressed and ends by exalting their values." They also overlook the point that the critic V. S. Pritchett has raised about Naipaul's work: "One does not ask a novelist to be absolutely true to life, in the sense of social or racial record; one asks him to be true to his design." In this, Naipaul is absolutely true. He is a superb journalist who has drawn his last novels from experiences previously spoken about as a reporter: Jimmy Ahmed inspired by Michael X, a Trinidadian Black power figure who murdered a white man; the Big Man is inspired by Zaïre's flamboyant President, Mobutu Sese Seko. His vision and design are fundamentally comic, his pessimism metaphysical. It has been said that one can never remember the final endings of great novels, but Naipaul's endings are always unforgettable, not as "freeze frames" but as epiphanies in which the whole book snaps into focus. The ending of his last novel is especially powerful as Salim leaves the beleaguered town at the bend of the river, he sees in the steamer's searchlight that a barge filled with less fortunate passengers has been left behind. "Then there were gunshots. The searchlight was turned off; the barge was no longer to be seen. The steamer started up again and moved without lights down the river, away from the area of battle. The air would have been full of moths and flying insects. The searchlight, while it was on, had shown thousands, white in the white light."

Naipaul has written about his admiration of Joseph Conrad for having made the same journeys before him, and he recently said: "It is remarkable that Conrad could look at the world with the utmost seriousness. What an achievement! Can you imagine the picture not to see it?" And so it is with Naipaul—though his sense of comedy is as dark as his seriousness. There is "charity" in even his darkest books—the charity of seeing. He refuses not to see.

His determination has not come easily. In Naipaul's books, as in his company, there is the sense of an opposing pull—into that withdrawal from the fray. Perhaps it is fear of giving in that brings such steel. His voice when he writes about India with its "self-cherishing in the midst of a general distress." His harsh 1977 report of a visit there, "India: A Wounded Civilization," is really an appeal to Indians to be more like *him*: "When men cannot observe, they don't have ideas; they have obsessions. When people live instinctive lives, something like a collective amnesia steadily blurs the past."

Some of Naipaul's best books have been the most painful to write. "*In a Free State* was written out of blood," he says. "I began it in Victoria, British Columbia, and after six weeks nothing happened. I always feel I scarcely deserve to have dinner or lunch when that happens. I even felt rebuked by the trees for bringing out their buds. It was written at my wife's aunt's house in Gloucester, very slowly written. I used to read the New English Bible aloud in the evenings to my wife—not the King James, which is liked by too many foolish people for that stupid rhythm and archaic language, which I *loathe*."

What part does his wife play in all this? "I read everything aloud to her as it's written—sometimes twice a day. It's my great weakness. But all my works, you know, are meant to be read aloud."

He wrote *Guerrillas* "in about five months of controlled frenzy. From then on I wrote and wrote. It just came. Until now. I very much hope to start something next year and write calmly for five or six years and then I'd like to stop." Why? "I've been working so hard—in my own mind since I was 9. All those scholarships! And writing is really such a *pressing* into the self—one longs to be liberated from it, really. I've developed a kind of ecstatic enjoyment of rest and looking. I'm very sorry the energy runs out—there are so many things to write about, so many big subjects."

That old specter of "emptiness" floats into view. Then he smiles: "All those modern Asiatics in the British Museum who spent a year in Seattle . . . Strange world! . . . Let's take a walk."

A Conversation with V. S. Naipaul

Bharati Mukherjee and Robert Boyers / 1981

From *Salmagundi* 54 (Fall 1981), 4–22. Reprinted by permission of *Salmagundi*.

Robert Boyers: *Somehow it seems strange to meet you here in this setting, in the sedate environs of a Wesleyan sitting room.*

V. S. Naipaul: I don't belong here, of course, although everyone has been very gracious. It's an intolerable place, really. Do you know that my students can't find a shop that sells the *New York Review of Books*? The college store apparently has never been asked by a member of the faculty to carry such a publication. I don't think you will find your own magazine here.

R.B.: *Still, the experience of teaching bright students must have its pleasures.*

VSN: Are they bright students? I don't know. I think it's bad to be mixing all the time with inferior minds. It's very, very damaging. To be with the young folk, the unformed mind, I think is damaging to one.

R.B.: *Where do you look for better minds? Where is your peer group?*

VSN: There are people. And you know, few things excite me more than meeting a man I admire.

R.B.: *Do you have a literary circle as such?*

VSN: No, but most of the people I know tend to be people who would be interested in my work, and have been for a long time. They are people whose interest I think is worth while.

Bharati Mukherjee: *One of the things you said years ago, I think, to Israel Shenker of the* New York Times, *I found very touching. You said that you write in London and don't have an audience, that you're just hanging in the air, doing the work of an artist in a vacuum, which is in a way absurd. You seemed to regret that you had no feedback. Do you feel that now, that sense of loss, that sense of insufficient feedback?*

VSN: It's diminishing. That is diminishing because I think I've got a kind of audience now. At least I'm read by other writers. But the problem is really very important, and very simple, isn't it? The writing of books, the publishing of books, may be taken for granted by people who belong to a society in which those activities are part of the social routine. Even

people who don't read books here know that there are other people who
do. They know that there are book shops. But I don't spring out of that
kind of society, and that is why I have felt that I am floating in a vacuum.
I am an oddity, and have always felt that I was an oddity, since I have
always been writing . . . I am an exotic to people who read my work, and
also to people who don't read it but know that is what I do. Asiatics do
not read, of course; they are a non-reading people. If they read at all,
they read for magic. They read holy books, they read sacred hymns, or
they read books of wisdom, books that will do them good. They do not
read for the sake of inquiry or curiosity because their religion has filled
the world for them completely. In the west, when you write you feel that
you write for a certain kind of individual. And you assume that readers
can feel themselves to be individuals. This is not an eternal in the world,
not a constant. To write a kind of literature that I can find interesting you
need to acquire an anxiety about man as an individual, and even in
Europe this is a relatively new thing. There are some "Asiatics" writing,
it is true. But they are recording for this outside audience their little tribal
rites and they're seen really not as new writers enlarging the sensibilities
of readers accustomed to works of real literary value.

    B.M.: *I am an extravagant admirer of your work and . . .*

    VSN: What do you find in it to admire?

    B.M.: *Well, you have articulated for people like me, for the first time,
a post-colonial consciousness without making it appear exotic. Your
writing is about unhousing and remaining unhoused and at the same time
free. I not only sympathize with that condition; I want to share that sense
of being cut off from a supporting world. But I'm also a little concerned
with, or perhaps I don't understand, your dismissal of the Asiatics and
their way of reading. Were you always as sure about Asians as you seem
now to be?*

    VSN: Well, in the first place I think that this word "Asian" is quite an
absurd word. It began to be used by Mr. Nehru in 1946 or '47 because,
he said, "Asiatic" was a weak word. The Japanese when they used it to
launch their propaganda in the 30's didn't think it was weak. Don't you
think that if the word earned a bit more respect it would be a lovely word?
Particularly as attached to a word like "prime" or "refined." That would
sound very nice. On the other hand, "prime Asiatic mind" doesn't say
as much to me as "dumb Asiatic mind." In any case, there is a sort of
connection between the two. I think, as you can see, that you must get
rid of the word "Asian" if you are to make your questions acceptable.

    B.M.: *But why should I be concerned about their being acceptable? I
only want you to tell us about your attitudes to third world readers. And*

it is a fact that not only "Asians"—or "asiatics"—but Africans read you . . .

VSN: No, I don't count the African readership and I don't think one should. Africa is a land of bush, again, not a very literary land. I don't see why it should get mixed up with Asia.

B.M.: *You are determined to be quarrelsome. Shall we just say, "non-white commonwealth" readership?*

VSN: That again is a very recent kind of division which I don't accept. You see, from the very early days I've been very careful in my work not to use words that produce the wrong associations. I don't use the word "imperialist" or "colonialist," for example. You say my work has some kind of meaning but you use words I can't use. In the 1950's those words or others like them might have had acceptable associations, but no longer. Now they are words that are used only by those chaps in the universities who made a specialty of putting things in political grooves. These are men who think they have a calling. They make investments in a political-academic stock market. Some are at present trading in African futures, creating a little calling . . . .

B.M.: *But the point I was trying to make, a point you intend obviously to obscure, is that you do have two groups of admirers. One group sees you not as part of any kind of ethnic or exotic literature but as voicing a kind of aloneness or lostness which is recognizably a part of a literary tradition. The other readers are trying to recognize, even identify with something that they think they've also experienced in their own lives.*

VSN: Yes, it's nice to think that there are readers who feel they can see their experience in what I've written. But finally the writer who thinks it's his business to get across the specificity of his material is making a great mistake. And I feel totally excluded by the works of writers like, shall we say, John Cheever, who are so much of their tribe that I think, as I read them, this is not for me, I mustn't enter there. I'm talking about what is really tribal literature, and I include in this even the stories of Hemingway, which can be quite good.

R.B.: *In this sense we can say that there has been a marked shift in your own work. The word* tribal *as you use it would seem much more applicable to a book like* A House For Mr. Biswas, *for example, than to any of the works of the last ten years.* Biswas *does have a certain particularizing inclination which is absent in the later novels. And it is plausible then to see the recent work as marking an advance, a maturity.*

VSN: Well yes, it's a good observation. Of course, when you're starting, you really have got to try to establish a world and it's much easier if you can even pretend that the tribal culture *is* a world, that the life of the street puts you in touch with the wider world. The early comedies made this pretense, I think, and they include *Biswas*, a book I think I remember, though I haven't read the book since I wrote it, you know. But even there, in a book like that, you can only pretend that you are totally shut in, that the condition is thoroughly imposed. You see that your goal is to get outside somehow by means of a tremendous intellectual exercise. I remember the anguish of those years, feeling always depleted. How was I to take the nature of my own life, which I couldn't refer to anything in my literary experience, and look for ways of entering the other life, a life led by people who would be strangers to one, people, say, living in London, with a history. It took me some years, even after I finished *Biswas*, to feel that I could do the job. I was still very shaky when I wrote *Mr. Stone*, the little book I wrote about England. Only after that did I really get going.

R.B.: *Did you know as you were writing* Mr. Biswas *that this was something that in a sense you had to see through but would leave behind as you moved on? Did you shape the future as you were moving through it?*

VSN: No, no, when one is writing one is always hoping at any stage to do it all, because—who knows?—you might die. You don't know, you never think about what's going to come next. I don't know what I'm going to do next year in my fiction. Even 8 months after I finish I'm just hoping that what I've written will lead on to something else.

B.M.: *In the early years, the anguish you describe must have had a lot to do with the absence of available literary models for works that like* Biswas *sought to render a world that had not really been done before.*

VSN: And of course for me this was complicated by the fact that I didn't even really belong in the exotic world I was born into and felt I had to write about. That life I wrote about in *Biswas* couldn't be the true nature of *my* life because I hadn't grown up in it feeling that it was mine. And that world itself was in fact turning when I entered it. How could one avoid the feeling of floating around? There are great mysteries in all this. It's a mystery that we in this room should all be talking the same language. And if I want to write about that mystery one thing I have to do is to avoid doing it in—here I'll use the word—in the way of the imperialist period novel. You know what I mean, the novel written by Hemingway or someone like that who always has the right passport and continues to pretend that it doesn't matter. But it would be quite different for someone like myself. I couldn't manage that pretense quite so easily.

R.B.: *There must be advantages in the condition you describe, though the disadvantages had to seem insurmountable at first.*

VSN: I will tell you. The good person, if he is dedicated, always makes his limitations into virtues. People looking at the work say, "God, you know, if only, if only, if only . . . ." That's true of me, too, I tend to complain of limitations. But there are virtues. Do you follow?

R.B.: *Yes, I think so.*

VSN: And there are after all financial limitations that are very much a part of this condition. I was just thinking about this today because for the first time in my life I actually sent off a note asking a magazine to commission a project. I've never done that before. I've always talked to people by word of mouth about ventures. I felt that my letter was a great humiliation after I posted it. And my mind went back to the utter humiliation I felt when my agent, who should have known better, made me take the manuscript of *Mr. Biswas* years ago to a hotel in London, where Mrs. Knopf of course rejected it instantly. They rejected the book because it was not publishable, and they were quite right, of course. It's not publishable because you don't write about Asiatics for a western audience which is in essence the only audience you can have. Such a book makes no commercial sense.

B.M.: *But how then have you seduced, persuaded the publishers? Including those who run the house of Knopf?*

VSN: By being around for a long time. Just by being around. I think it's fair in some ways. If you've been around for 25 years as a writer it means that there probably is something there. It isn't someone simply going through a phase or responding to a passing provocation. I've sat out the Forster thing about relationships and a great many other temptations. You know how easy it would have been for me to subscribe to the pretentious stuff. How many people would have liked me to take as my slogan "only connect," that sort of thing. What other sort of things have I sat out? When I was young there was Kafka. But those temptations are gone.

R.B.: *It's very interesting to go back to the reviews, and when you do, you find it's not always easy to understand why you should have had trouble. In general the reviews were very favorable, and the books were respectfully treated even in the major reviews.*

VSN: Which ones? The American or British?

R.B.: *American and British reviews, in fact. There were favorable early notices in the* New York Times, *in* Encounter, *and so on. Yet, as you say, it has taken considerable time for the impact to be felt—in the U.S. especially. It's a very curious thing to me . . . I can't think of any other writer so favorably and fairly reviewed who had to write so long for a readership.*

VSN: My books here used to sell six or seven hundred copies, you know.

R.B.: *Yes, it's incredible.*

VSN: Maybe libraries bought them.

R.B.: *Do you feel that you've educated your audience? Have you created the audience that now reads the unpublishable books like Biswas?*

VSN: No, I think it's all due to a number of very good, kind and generous people who have liked my work over the years, ever since I have been writing. I think it's entirely due to them, not to me.

R.B.: *May we speak some more about your "origins"? Some time ago, you wrote about Conrad, and I am quoting: "Conrad's value to me is that he is someone who, 60 to 70 years ago, meditated on my world, a world I recognize today. I feel this about no other writer of the century . . ." Would you talk a little about this?*

VSN: Oh yes, I'll tell you what I mean. I had a lot of trouble with Conrad when I was young because I read his work as a sign of what a novel should really entail—the psychological truth, etc. Conrad had a way of playing the fool in many ways, with his specious dramatizations. His cinematic eye often got him in a lot of trouble. I really don't think he has all the fine gifts of a novelist—doesn't have the true fantasy of a novelist. But in a practical way I cannot imagine Virginia Woolf or Proust or any of the other writers we admire considering the world I come from as being of any value. It is remarkable that Conrad could look at that world with the utmost seriousness. What an achievement! Can you imagine the pressure not to see it? Asiatics are people that simply didn't exist as individuals. In the novel of the 19th century they are just background, never more. Well, what a wonderful thing to do, to study the difference between two different kinds of people. With Conrad you have a great effort of understanding, of sympathy—do you feel that?

R.B.: *What you say is really intriguing, since I have had the impression you resented Conrad.*

VSN: When I was young I did actually say—I think it was in *The Times* of 1962—that I couldn't get on with Conrad.

R.B.: *You went so far as to say that what you found "peculiar but depressing" about Conrad is that he comes to the fiction with ready made conclusions, where Ibsen's writing seemed a lot more exciting.*

VSN: Yes, I still think there is much that is depressing in Conrad's writing. He begins very late, remember, he marries a lady who turns very fashionable, and he has all sorts of pressures on his time. He finds it necessary to churn out tales, tales. And his talent really never should have gone to producing all those tales. I find that very, very depressing. It is the wisdom that is not depressing. I believe he began to publish at about 38, though he began to write years before. So he was really very, very wise by the time he came to do the things most of us know.

B.M.: *Are there any living writers you find exciting or wise in the same way? Writers whose work reflects the anxiety about change and an absorption in essential questions that you find bracing?*

VSN: I know that literary intellectuals have a capacity to become excited about what's coming up next. I don't, and so I have a harder time than you in admiring current writers. Most of them seem to me terribly conventional. This doesn't mean that good ones don't exist. But who are they? I think that many recent writers have shared this view of mine, that even the better writers are perhaps missing the essence. I don't actually know all that many new American writers. Do you think I'm wrong?

R.B.: *It's hard to say. We'd have to define what we mean by "essence," and we'd have to identify the different kinds of novels produced in this country. And that won't be fruitful here. But what of the current English novel?*

VSN: I can't be interested in the latest English extravaganza. I can't be interested in a novel about the men in London. I can't—It's too far from me.

R.B.: *That's too bad in a way. Since quite obviously that is what many American and English readers have said to you. They can't be interested in a novel about the people in Africa or the Caribbean. They're "too far" from us.*

VSN: Yes, well one has one's limitations, and there it is. But I continue to think there is a difference here. I feel that the most interesting books have a certain instability about them which I don't find in current English fiction.

R.B.: *An instability? I'm not sure I know what you mean. I suppose you mean something about the content of the work. And in this sense maybe it is someone like Orwell you'd prefer to the current crop.*

VSN: Yes, Orwell remains very interesting, doesn't he? To break away from the stable English phase he had to pretend that he was a pauper. He had to learn to strip himself of all his earliest assumptions. He is the most imaginative writer, most imaginative man in English history. He travelled in a new direction. Don't you agree?

R.B.: *I must confess that to me Orwell is most appealing as an essayist, a journalist—much more so than as a novelist.*

VSN: The novels also are interesting. But whichever of his works you prefer, he does not write like the English writers I know. What I miss is the novels of London life, as also in the novels of suburban misery, is the instability. In them you have the assumption of being, that what is, has already been, and will continue. The Soviets too write most often about what is constant. I much prefer writers who can carry in their writing some sense of what is, wasn't always, has been made, and is about to change again and become something else.

R.B.: *Orwell, of course, spent a good deal of time writing journalism, and so have you. Would you tell us a little bit about how journalism feeds into your fiction?*

VSN: I'm getting too old to do it well, you know, though journalism is something that engages me and in a sense keeps me going. Those articles—many of them—called up the most complex skills. They required that I hold myself open for encounters, for adventures, that I always be alert without knowing what next to look out for. They had me wondering always what questions to ask, how to get on with people, how to let people talk. I had to learn to understand what would prejudice my grasp of any given country or situation, and I worked to acquire a travel skill that would let me know when the time had come for me to go away, to know when things had begun to repeat themselves. After a while you've got the material, but the writing is always altering that material. You've got to be alert to the various pressures, all the temptations to draw social lessons. Everything you know is engaged. It's a total exercise. I think it's the most difficult, the most complete thing you can do.

R.B.: *Do you feel that the vision of things you arrive at in that way is very different from the conclusions you reach in the fiction?*

VSN: They come out of two entirely different segments of the brain. And they're actually written differently. I just mentioned this to someone else the other day. The fiction begins on the typewriter, which allows when necessary for a certain speed, if there is anything there. The other has to be done very carefully, so it's done by hand, because it's very planned, you know? Have you ever had the experience of sort of picking your way around? You land in the airport and you stand there and ask yourself: What shall I do? Anything that begins that way is going to take shape very differently from a work of fiction. But the reporting helped me to study the world, helped me a lot really, though it was a great strain, a great effort when I began doing it.

B.M.: *It has been said about some of the non-fiction—I'm thinking especially of* The Middle Passage—*that . . .*

VSN: That was the first one. *The Middle Passage*—yes, a very funny book. I continue to like it a great deal.

B.M.: *But it was said, when it appeared, that you were approaching*

*the country with preconceived conclusions—that you went to confirm
expectations rather than to explore what was before you.*

VSN: Yes, there were complaints. In the 1960's people were shouting
for certain political movements in those places I visited, so when I
stepped in to say that this is stupid, that this is just routine, nothing more
than public affairs, those who were shouting did not approve. By now of
course I think they've given up. The particular holy man they were
pushing at the time in those places has been abandoned. And you know,
I think that the books of real writers, even when they are reporter's
books, must be judged on their ability to stand up. A writer's book has to
stand even after the events have changed. My book was written in '61,
published in '62. So 18 years later it has to stand up or not. You read it
now and I think you see that it's fair—it's fair. Or is it not fair? But
obviously it offended people who had their own prejudices, who thought
that shouting racist slogans in 1960 was wonderful. I thought they were
horrible.

B.M.: *But it has been said of* The Middle Passage *that you . . .*

VSN: If *The Middle Passage* is found untrue today, 18 years later, then
I will debate what seems untrue. If it remains true, if you cannot bring
yourself to say, 'You were wrong here, and here, or here,' then there is
no sense asking how I came to arrive at these things. I arrived at them
because I refused to go in with preconceived notions. You know, people
are always convinced that their political passion is wonderful, and then
surprised when they find they've learned nothing from their experiences.
You must read the book, and tell me that the chapter on Jamaica is not
marvelously prescient, pre-visionary of what has happened lately. If you
can tell me that, *then* attack me. Don't tell me otherwise that I shouldn't
have said what I say about the illiterate black man shouting for racial
redemption and found to get nowhere. Will you say they have gotten
somewhere? I'll say they've gotten nowhere. They've destroyed their
little world. I say they've taken several large steps back to the bush. And
it's surprised me. I never thought that after 300 years of the new world
an African people could return to the bush. That is very sad.

B.M.: *What is amazing to me is the confidence with which you can say
that the objective truth is they have returned to the bush.*

VSN: I'm being very provocative, but I'm also speaking with a lot of
bitterness. And much unhappiness. Because it is not pleasant to see the
place where you were born destroyed, and that is the bottom of it. There
are no institutions, nothing to refer to any longer. You cannot refer to any
idea of law, or honesty about public money or the rights of all men,
because racialist politics in a way rejects all these values. And I wish that

people would see that in fact one is really bitter because of the collapse of human values. *I'm* not fighting a racial war; the people who ban me over there are fighting a racial war. And that is a sign of the collapse of civilization, of the possibility of movement forward.

B.M.: *This revelation of the bitterness behind the easy generalization that . . .*

VSN: Easy generalization? It's taken a long time to think about the bush. It's a big thing, there is no easy generalization or easy conclusion. It's as difficult as the conclusion you come to after being in India. It takes a long time in India to come to the simple conclusion that, by God, these people are just extraordinarily stupid! There is no hidden virtue in a man like Desai. There is no secret intelligence in these people. The people running the country and playing politics are just very, very stupid. Now *that's* a breakthrough, since these simple things elude one; because one is so full of received ideas one just doesn't see the truth.

R.B.: *But why haven't you applied this kind of soul-searching and possible breakthrough of insight to British society, too? You haven't really dealt with England except in the early novel, have you?*

VSN: That's right.

B.M.: *And if you were to turn your whole intellectual machinery on the English, would they also be likely to come up seeming incredibly stupid?*

VSN: They are in trouble. And it's the trouble that comes to every country that has really been tremendously successful. There have been few countries as successful as England in the world—and not successful only in one way but in almost all ways, except perhaps painting and music. This of English literature, science, the institutions of law and government, their establishing the right of man, their prodigious history. Have you read Darwin? Isn't it marvelous? As a young man I read *The Voyage of the Beagle*, and I thought, how wonderful that a young man who was a scientist, not a writer by profession, could write so magnificently.

B.M.: *I think of Darwin and Freud and a number of others as literature, not as theory or science.*

VSN: I think the finest English minds can be found outside the purely literary enterprise. But you know, great vanity can set in when a people are so successful. They begin to believe in racial magic, and finally exalt the form rather than the substance. Darwin's great because Darwin is, well . . . Darwin, but eventually he just becomes part of English Literature. And the general achievement extends then to manner of speaking, manner of addressing, to the shadow, the shadow, and a great tradition

How about
Jessie Boot

goes quickly into its decline. You can see it here in America. I'm sure
that the fathers of the current student generation here had some feeling
that it was necessary for them to work and achieve something. Already,
in one generation after the consolidation of America's undoubted domi-
nance in the world, you have people who are unlettered, extraordinarily
vain, lazy, corrupt but at places like Wesleyan at least they take great
care to dress the correct "preppy" way. The thing that they are *not*
interested in is work or achievement. A great success begins to breed a
kind of corrupting vanity. I'm afraid it's quite common in human society.

B.M.: *Of course you are chiefly interested in another kind of society,
a world largely unfamiliar to British and American audiences. For me,
Mr.* Biswas *was a really exciting breakthrough because it went from the
closed communal satire of the communal world to the study of unhousing
and housing. But there were problems you had to solve in all the early
works. How did you, in the early novels, get across to the foreign
audience the necessary sense of a wife-beating hero coming from a wife-
beating culture? Your audience really couldn't know how to respond to a
hero who is also a wife-beater. In a Cheever novel, if a character beats
his wife, we know he is a bad guy. For you the situation had to be
very different.*

VSN: Well, I think of the words I used to describe that wife-beating. I
said that it made them very close, or something like that. I've forgotten
the sentence, which was written some years ago—23, I think. I remember
it stuck in my mind, and I thought it might remain with others too.

B.M.: *Yes, it was a memorable sentence. But, you see, that particular
paragraph is a little troubling, because there's an easy assumption there
about the couple's having fallen into their roles. Everything was comfortable, you suggest, the wife had been beaten, and each of them had
fulfilled his assigned roles. I think that* that *kind of easy assumption—you
won't like that phrase "easy assumption"—is no longer possible in
your fiction.*

VSN: Not at all. Absolutely. You can no longer do that. Everybody,
everything has to be explained very carefully. But when you do that sort
of subject, well, you find it's an unavoidably funny subject, no matter
how you try to explain it. You know the joke: Do you still beat your wife?
But the treatment of the subject needn't be malicious. It's a serious thing.
Wife-beating is very prevalent, as I found out when I went to the courts
and followed all the cases. One afternoon in my hotel I met one of these
men. And I said: Do you really beat your wife?—and he said, I don't, but
my neighbor does. These things can be very funny, but you can't always
be sure your reader will take them in as you'd like.

R.B.: *Do you consider the audience when you work out a scene or a crucial detail in your novels? I'm speaking, for example, of the scene in* Guerrillas *in which the very unlovely young woman is brutally sodomized. In drafting such a scene, would it be necessary for you to imagine the response of the reader, and perhaps to modify the treatment of that episode accordingly?*

VSN: Yes, of course. I had to be careful. The novel, you know, hangs between two sexual scenes. The first explains the second. I was very nervous before I wrote the first one. And I was appalled by the second. I hope I was careful enough to remove from the sex scenes any association of the standard erotic writing. But I was appalled. Yet I couldn't remove all of the more erotic or excitatory associations of words. I know it's offended a lot of people. It really has. But you see, the terror of that book is inevitable. It's a book about lies and self deception and people inhabiting different worlds or cultures. It is the only book I know which is really about an act of murder. That is why it's shocking—and the fact that it shocks you is part of its success. But it's the wrong kind of success if you just think, God she was such an unpleasant girl. If she was really all that unpleasant, if you hadn't been made to understand her, you wouldn't have found her death to be so appalling.

R.B.: *Were you surprised at the very favorable reception of the book in the United States?*

VSN: The book lost me about half my readership in England. They couldn't take it.

R.B.: *It's very strong medicine. But I was surprised, again, that someone like Hilton Kramer thought so very highly of the book. I would've thought that . . . .*

VSN: I think he responded to the pain in the book, and to the fact that it's a moralistic book. It has very hard things to say about people who play at serious things, who think they can always escape, run back to their safe world. The woman in the novel is a study in vanity, and perhaps people like Kramer have strong feelings about that kind of vanity.

R.B.: *You describe* Guerrillas *as a moralistic book. Do you then see yourself as having moved resolutely from satire into moral fiction?*

VSN: I want to go back to comedy now. Oh yes, I want to go back to comedy. Having gone through those dark things, and drawing upon all my knowledge, I want to be funny once again. Why not? Why shouldn't one be funny?

R.B.: *Would you describe your latest novel,* A Bend in the River, *as a comedy?*

VSN: Well, I think it's a little funnier than the other book.

B.M.: *It can't be funnier than* Guerrillas*! Can it?*

VSN: Do you know *Guerrillas* is full of jokes? If I had read *Guerrillas* aloud you would be roaring with laughter. Really.

R.B.: *This is something I'll have to think about. To accept what you say here would commit me to a separation of form and content that I'm not comfortable about. Though this would place you, in a way, closer to some of the more reflexive or self-regarding writers of contemporary fiction, who are not primarily "writing about," but "writing." Do you have any kind of interest at all in the kind of fiction we associate with writers like Donald Barthelme or William Gass? There seem to be a great many more prominent novelists of that kind in the United States than elsewhere.*

VSN: How would you define their work?

R.B.: *I sense that you are asking because you don't ordinarily read books by such writers. And of course there are drastic differences between a Gass and a Barthelme. For one such writer what counts more than anything else is a love of language for its own sake. For another what counts is the calling into being of the play function of the mind. In any of these writers the element of signification is decidedly modest. They disdain, for themselves, the representational possibilities of fiction.*

VSN: I think it's a legitimate thing to do.

B.M.: *You think this is a legitimate option for an unhoused writer?*

VSN: To play with language?

B.M.: *Yes. To be a Nabokov . . .*

VSN: Oh yes, for any writer, I think it's quite legitimate. Whether it's satisfactory in the long run is another matter, but it's quite legitimate. I wouldn't run it down. I recognize it as one of the twists of the world, you know.

R.B.: *You don't have the sense that the novel today has a specific function, a job of work to do . . . nothing of that sort. That's to the good, so far as I am concerned. And really what you say confirms my sense of* In a Free State, *or at least the sense of it I got when I reread it a few weeks ago. I found there a wonderful subversive quality, if I may use that term, a quality found only in fictions that deal with plausibly human persons, but which undermine all ordinary expectations attaching to familiar representations. Here you have two people on their way to a particular place, in a car, and a windshield which can be scratched the way it might be scratched in a naturalistic fiction. But one accepts at once in reading the novel that that isn't at all the level at which one is interested. One isn't interested at all in the scratch on the windshield or in the destination to which the car is headed, one is interested really in* *the way in which our familiar relation to the world is threatened. Nothing more than that. I have the sense that in the book what is real is the sense of menace. None of the particulars attaching to that menace matter. Does that make sense?*

VSN: That was a very, very hard book to write. There is dialogue all the way through, and for that to work you have to establish the lives and relationships of all the people precisely. But you also have to get what is happening outside. Even the history of the land plays an important part. You stress the dramatic arrangement, I think. But when you stress that you say in effect that you don't feel that it's real, that the land is real.

R.B.: *I didn't feel that as in any way a lack, a failure. For me the book aims at, and achieves, a negation of concreteness, a negation of real options, of the ordinary, and in that sense for me it is the most potent of all your works, though not the most appealing.*

VSN: Oh, but I had them rolling in the aisles last week when I read in New York from the restaurant sequence. Though later on they were a little shocked to discover they were laughing at something people shouldn't really be laughing at. It was too late for them to regret their laughter.

R.B.: *But even the humor there seems to be of a very special sort. It's not satirical in the way one expects from earlier books.*

VSN: I agree it is an odd book. But of course one can't analyze one's work.

B.M.: *To me it was terrifying, not only because of the terror of the situation, but because of the vision which said all politics is silly, and the African people will necessarily revert to the bush.*

VSN: You know, I began to write the book in '69, before anyone can have seen exactly how accurate my predictions would be. I got a fabulous roasting when the book came out in 1971. Our African "strong man" hadn't really shown his hand then. The book offended a lot of people who just couldn't visualize the developments in a land like Uganda, which I drew with touches of Kenya and one or two other countries. My critics didn't see what could happen with someone who's kicked out the Asiatics and put the Europeans under seige. I was thinking again the other day how I got very frightened being there in 1966. I used to think, "I'm alone here . . . terrible things are coming here." But I could not have worked out the means by which in that pacific, lovely place, where people are so gentle and nice, there would suddenly be guns and killing and the prisons would be full of blood.

R.B.: *Does your political passion lead you to read the newspapers every day? You sound like a man who needs to stay on top of events.*

VSN: That's the trouble. Though I used to have an appetite for the papers when I was younger, I came to feel that they're unhealthy. They're bad for you like eating ice cream for breakfast, lunch and dinner. And they tell you nothing new. I spend more time on the news magazines. There are a number of good ones in this country.

B.M.: *Can you tell me more about politics you are most interested in?*

VSN: I'll tell you a little story, though I won't mention names. There's an elegant lady in England . . . getting on now. She wrote a novel about a lady with a lover; the lady had a moral crisis—"Would I condemn others when I'm immoral . . . ," you know that kind of thing, all very delicate and beautiful. And this novel came out a few days before the pound took its enormous dive—it seemed it was going to touch one dollar fifty. And I thought, the dive of the pound—that extended event—has destroyed the value of this novel, which implies that this world is of value, that values are steady and are going to go on. But when your pound crashes, you cannot make those assumptions any more.

B.M.: *Your story in a way addresses our earlier question about writers like Barthelme.*

VSN: Well yes, I suppose all that assumes great security, that the world is going on; and that I can't assume, you see.

R.B.: *Perhaps you insist too much that all is hopeless, that nothing can come from India or from other places in the third world. And perhaps you are mistaken when you say that European methods of historical inquiry "cannot be applied to Indian Civilization."*

VSN: Clearly you have read Indian history. And so you must know that there are all sorts of things no Western historian can know what to do with.

B.M.: *You say this over and over again, but I don't see that you've really made a case.*

VSN: You think it can be done?

B.M.: *Yes. And I guess the other problem that I have with your kind of vision is dismissal of the passions of people in these far-off places. I know it's absurd to be born in Calcutta or in Port of Spain . . . but it hurts those of us who have had that misfortune to hear you talk of it as you do.*

VSN: Do I dismiss that passion?

B.M.: *Well, to say that these people are incapable of serious thought on their own condition, or that they don't deserve a sympathetic and serious voice is, I think, tantamount to dismissal.*

VSN: They've had too much sympathy, don't you think? They've had too many lovers of India loving them for their wretchedness and their misery and their slavery and their wish to keep others trapped.

B.M.: *But no one I know wants to encourage that kind of Indophile.*

VSN: Who do you want? You see, I'm not sure you know. What I want is for India to regard itself as a big country. It should be doing something in the world. It should have high standards of achievement. A country with 600 to 700 million people which is now offering the world nothing but illegitimate holy men should be ashamed of itself. And if that's the stupidity you've arrived at then you really should pull yourself up and say, "What can we do about it?" For a time I hoped my little proddings might start something. But clearly they're not going to start anything at all. And I do want you to see that I don't dismiss them because they're too far away. I'm very sad they've made themselves so negligible in the world. I think they pay a bitter price for being negligible. And I wish they could see that for themselves.

B.M.: *Your books, then, really grow out of pain and irritation . . .*

VSN: And a concern . . .

B.M.: *Rather than contempt.*

VSN: Oh, concern, oh certainly. One can't write out of contempt. If you try to do that, the book won't survive and won't irritate. Contempt can be ignored. But let's go back to your point about European methods applied to something as bizarre as Hindu history. Consider that in a way Hindu civilization stopped growing a long time ago. Nothing has been happening except plunder, war, decimation.

R.B.: *But truly the alternative would not be to write the history from within Hindu culture. That cannot be what you propose. Said of course argues that to write about the Orient, one must entirely abandon any presumption of objectivity. One must, to do the job, write from a position of advocacy, from within. Only in this way will one want to do justice to one's subject. I don't see how this can be your view.*

VSN: I think that any Hindu of intelligence who saw his history would be so appalled he would decide to go do something about it. And since things just go on as always, the Hindus must not see.

R.B.: *Again, that's why I was curious about your rejection of European methods of historical analysis.*

VSN: I'm not trying to reject, but to inquire. Let's think: Can you write a satisfactory history of England from the pre-Roman time up through the Roman occupation, the Roman withdrawal, the time of the little savage kings, and their being wiped out by the Danes—the consequence of all this being that nothing happened? It wouldn't make sense to write weighty histories about that; whereas, if you make all this a chapter of something larger, the material conceivably can stand that kind of inquiry. Remember what I wrote years ago, that history was built around achievement and creation.

R.B.: *And in this sense, one might say, no form of history will presumably do justice to the complexities. They will require some other form entirely . . .*

VSN: Probably something else is needed. Probably. As long as the same little things keep happening over and over again, with the same pointless stops and starts.

R.B.: *But more seems to be involved here than the repudiation of particular historical forms. In* The Mimic Men *the narrator fails to see what good can come to the effort to put oneself in the place of those who are distressed. The effort, he concludes, we can make only "when we seek to forget ourselves by taking on the burden of others."*

VSN: Did I write that?

R.B.: *I think I've got it right. At least that's what your narrator says.*

VSN: I wrote those words?

R.B.: *Yes, you did.*

VSN: Sometimes I forget, you know. But read it again for me, will you?

R.B.: *He "tried to put myself in the place of those I thought were distressed. In so doing, he concludes, 'I failed to see much. I minimized the quality of personality. But so it is when we seek to forget ourselves by taking on the burden of others.' " To what degree can the narrator in that novel be said to speak for you?*

VSN: No, no, no. That isn't *me*. In fact, I had the other view, that there is more to people than their distress. That they are real people. And unless you understand that everyone has cause for self-esteem, you make a terrible political error. The marxists tend to reduce people to their distress, or to their economic position. It's the sort of thing Conrad observes a little bit in The Secret Agent. He has another way of saying everyone has a cause for self-esteem. Everyone has something outside himself which gives him some idea of his own status. But you can't assume that people who live in a bleak condition have nothing at all to esteem in themselves, and will therefore answer any revolutionary call at all.

R.B.: *May I shift ground a bit? In a review of* An Area of Darkness, *a well-known British critic makes some rather critical observations about the book. But then he goes on to say that the book has a great many strengths, and that it is, finally, "wonderfully enjoyable." Do you think that a satisfactory conclusion for a critic, or a reader?*

VSN: I think it's entirely satisfactory. I think books should be fun. I think what is wrong with a writer like Conrad, for all his brilliance, is that you don't rush home and say, "Now I'm going to settle down and read a wonderful book." This is what you do for Balzac and for Tolstoy. And if this is good for them, why shouldn't we demand it from the rest of us?

B.M.: *And you feel the same way about non-fiction? That its primary responsibility is, as it were, to be enjoyable?*

VSN: There might be instances in which this response would not be appropriate. But I'm willing to believe that the element of pleasure is almost invariably paramount.

V. S. Naipaul:
A Perpetual Voyager

Bernard Levin / 1983

From *The Listener*, 23 June 1983, 16–17. Reprinted by permission of Bernard Levin and Curtis Brown.

Bernard Levin: *You were born in Trinidad?*

V. S. Naipaul: I was born there, yes. I thought it was a great mistake.

How early did you start thinking that?

Quite early. I just wanted to go to a prettier place. I didn't like the climate. I didn't like the quality of the light. I didn't like the heat; I didn't like the asthma that gave me. I didn't like a lot of the racial tensions around me. These were connected as much with Africans as with Europeans. I wanted to be free of all that. I didn't like the music; I didn't like the loudness. I just felt I was in the wrong place.

You presumably were surrounded by your family, which was entirely Indian?

Yes, but I'm talking about the world outside as well, I didn't like my family particularly either. To grow up in a large, extended family was to acquire a lasting distaste for family life. It was to give me the desire never to have any children of my own. Then, from another source within the family, I developed a feeling for things of beauty, for good manners, for writing, and I developed a fantasy, I suppose, of civilisation as something existing away from this area of barbarity. The barbarity was double: the barbarity of my family and the barbarity outside.

Forgive me if I'm pressing on an old wound, but you say the barbarity of your family. What was barbarous about it?

I would have preferred greater graciousness; I would have preferred greater qualities of mind; I also would have preferred greater generosity of spirit. I grew up among people who endlessly made moral judgments about behaviour and so they were full of jealousies and malice because there was nothing else for them. You see, I think that the Hindu attitude, like the attitudes of many Eastern religions, is profoundly materialist. I think that disinterested acts and attitudes to certain things being good in themselves for their own sake—like not to be cruel, like to be kind—come

93

from self-aware, highly civilised societies. I don't think they come from ritualised cultures.

You mentioned one particular source you said, to things of beauty, among other things.

That, of course, was my father. He was a journalist and I think that probably without his presence and probably without his genes I would have been different. I would probably just have lived and accepted.

Did you conceive the ambition to be a writer early?
Very, very early; I was about ten or 11.

From your father's example, as it were?

Yes, from that. And at really quite an early age I thought of myself as a writer. What is interesting about this is that it didn't go with any wish to write a particular thing; it didn't go with the discovery of any particular talent when I was a child. It was just something that was given to me as a fantasy of nobility, a fantasy of the good life, the beautiful life, the civilised life. I became a writer because of this overwhelming idea of its nobility as a calling, which was given to me by my father and probably exaggerated by me. I feel when I talk to people whose attitude to writing is not quite like mine—good writers, who are more matter of fact and might even think of books as properties—that I was over-serious, and have been over-serious. But it is really too late for me to change now.

You make it sound like a vocation.

That is the word. I think that if I hadn't succeeded in being a writer I probably would not have been around; I would have done away with myself in some way.

Did writing come easily?

No, everything had to be learnt, because to write a paragraph of narrative prose is quite different from writing a paragraph in a school or university essay. I remember my father reading to me when I was about ten the first line of a novel by a successful romantic writer called Warwick Deeping. The novel was called *Smith* and the first line, I believe, was: 'Three men were at work in the carpenter's shop.' My father told me: 'Now, that's a beautiful line, that's the way to begin a piece of writing.' This idea about the way you handle words and the feeling for words is something I had to learn after getting rid of the academic style of school and university. I also had to learn how to organise material—the most difficult thing about writing. There is a large organisation of material, then there is a smaller assemblage: the paragraphs, the links, the prepara-

tion of what is coming on after—very, very involved. Then the tensions
that narrative prose must have; occasionally, perhaps, the rhetoric. I find
it a very tiring, taxing art, but it is the one that I do.

*At what point, if there was one, did you feel that you had achieved
something worth while and would go on doing so?*
I felt I'd done something when I was about 28 or 29. I managed to get
into a fairly large book and I wrote it with complete conviction and I felt
I had done something, I felt taken out of myself. I felt that the vocation,
which didn't come from any natural gift—the craft had to be learnt—had
somehow taken off. Achievement—I don't have any sense of
achievement.

You sound as though writing itself gives you very little joy.
Forster did say people usually say that about writing—but he enjoyed
writing. If you were in flow, if you were writing a book and things were
moving, one might have that feeling one day in the week, one short day.
If they weren't, it can spoil your day; you really can feel that you can't
enjoy anything.

*Well, there's certainly a lot of what you are saying now in your books.
May I quote a sentence from one of your books that I find quite haunting?
It's the opening sentence of* A Bend in the River, *which, if I may remind
you, begins: 'The world is what it is; men who are nothing, who allow
themselves to become nothing, have no place in it.' That's a very severe,
Jehovah-like judgment on the world, is it not? Or, at any rate, on those
millions who have nothing, who are nothing, who allow themselves to
become nothing, the weak, the feeble, the failures. It's a stern judgment,
I can't help thinking.*
I don't think it is an admirable thing to live an instinctive life, as some
people do in some cultures. I don't think it is an admirable thing to be
placid, or lazy, or not to express oneself fully. I don't see how such
people can expect to win regard.

But an awful lot of people DON'T expect to win regard.
I can't understand that kind of person. Probably it's my nature. I like
people who want to do things. I like people who want to do things
very well.

*Well, of course, the heroes of your novels, again and again, are the
strivers, aren't they?—those who strive and who define themselves. I
can't help feeling that, somewhere out of the corner of your eye, there's
a great void in which you fear to fall.*

I think, if you don't strive, then the mind is unengaged and, if the mind is unengaged, then life must be a little worthless.

But aren't we condemning nine-tenths of the human race in this airy fashion?
Not airy. It's open to anybody to do, to act. I think it's wrong of people to say that they don't act, they don't do, and that therefore they are entitled to consideration simply because they *are*; I think they should earn interest at any rate, and they should deserve our regard and our compassion. I don't think people are entitled to it simply because they're here.

Did you feel this very strongly when you made your pilgrimage back to the place in India where your forebears came from?
I think the Indians are very active, very energetic; they have a great scientific revolution. Industrially, they've done very well, and this is now bearing intellectual fruit—the quality of their newspapers has gone up, the level of the intellectual life in India has also gone up, the quality of discussion has gone up. I think, through this contact with the technological society, they have become rather more humanised. Society is beginning to humanise itself.

This is an amazing judgment on India, that India, in Forster's phrase, 'whose only peer was the Holy Roman Empire.' Shall she in the latter day achieve it through the technological revolution? You sit there and tell me that?
Absolutely. The machine is the great humaniser of those societies. It gives men whose labours have been very petty a new idea of themselves and their skills. And I think people in India who use the machines actually do like the machines. This is probably true also of Asia. This is probably why Asia is so good with machines. Men have got new ideas of themselves, not through philosophy, or philosophers' thinking over generations, but through using a wonderful machine, which produces lovely goods, which makes them admire and regard themselves more highly.

But that is a very material universe, is it not?
In religions like Hinduism and Buddhism there are no disinterested acts. Charity is not to be exercised for its own sake, there is always a reward. You are kind not because man is your fellow, you are kind because there is perhaps some reward. You exchange virtue for goods. It is only in this other civilisation that you have the idea of the good act in itself or the attitude to men because they are men and therefore your fellows. In other religions, in the East, it might be that you have a feeling

only for the man of your tribe or of your faith—he might be your brother.
Everybody else is not your brother.

*Do you mean, then, that altruism, since that's what we're talking
about, is a European concept, not a human concept?*

I think it probably is a concept of the Renaissance European world. I
haven't found it in India, I haven't found it among Indians. If you study
Gandhi, for instance, everything that Indians think of as Indian in Gandhi
is really Victorian, acquired by contact with Victorian England. Interest-
ingly, Gandhi, in his autobiography, says that it was Christianity when he
was in South Africa that kept alive religion in him. Another interesting
thing he says is that when he was about to renounce the world, in 1910,
he worried about it and then his training as a lawyer came to his help. He
thought of Snell's *Equity* and the idea of trusteeship came to him: man
was thus then a trustee. You find throughout the early part of Gandhi's
autobiography that it is permeated with Victorian learning and Victorian
ideals, and Western ideals—the ideals of the other civilisation.

*We're accustomed to think today, aren't we, that Europe imposed
European culture, European attitudes, 'Europeanism,' on peoples for
whom it was not a plant that could be grafted and that that is where the
trouble—the modern world—began. You seem to deny that utterly.*

I do think that the world is culturally and spiritually very, very, varied,
and the appearance of the homogeneous world is a delusion that men do
inhabit within their cultures special intellectual and spiritual words. There
is a good deal of misunderstanding of one group by another because of
this appearance that we might be talking about the same thing, or that we
all have the same goals. In West Africa, for instance, I don't think the
idea of development, or law, or democracy, is as important as the defeat
of sorcery. It's much more important to wipe out completely sorcery
from the world, dispel the evil spirit, by whatever means, than to have
roads or to elect your own president.

*But is it possible to drive out sorcery without the other weapons of the
modern world: your roads and your presidents and your elections?*

I'm talking about a specific country now, a country in West Africa
where the experiment that is being done is to drive sorcery out by
traditional methods. The President possesses good magic, so it is possible
to defeat sorcery by good magic.

*You seem to me—not, I think, only because you have travelled so
widely—to be a kind of perpetual voyager through this world, who does
not put down roots.*

I don't think any of us can claim that we come from one single, enclosed, tribal world. We are little, bombarded cells, aren't we?—many things occur to make us what we are, and we can surely live with all the things that make us.

We can live with them, but where do we feel at home is the question that must present itself to us.

I think that that presents itself to me. I solve the problem by travelling and when I get tired I know I can move on. I don't think about it now as a problem. I just move.

Moving on seems to be something you have done all your life, in one sense or another.

Moving on and moving back, moving on and moving back. I think many people find themselves in that position.

What will you move on to next?

I don't know. One is getting a little tired, one will probably stay fixed for a bit.

Fixed geographically perhaps, but not fixed intellectually, I think let alone artistically.

No. I would like to do some comic novels before I finish. My early gift, my early talent, the way I expressed myself most easily when I began to write, was in the comic form and then because of one's exploration of the world and the world changing around one—one didn't make the jokes, the jokes were there. I would like to return, in maturity, to that comic view.

But not set in the Caribbean?

No, that's 33 years ago. The difficulty of a writing career like mine is that, creatively and imaginatively, I've had to incorporate not only my own developing experience, changing world, but the fact that one had moved out of one place. Most people find it best to write about enclosed societies. Most television serials are about closed communities: whether they're post office people or people at a police station, it's much easier to write about an enclosed world. To write about a world which is much more shattered, and exploding, and varied, write about it in fiction, is very difficult.

V. S. vs the Rest: The Fierce and Enigmatic V. S. Naipaul Grants a Rare Interview in London

James Atlas / 1987

From *Vanity Fair*, March 1987, 66, 68. Reprinted by permission of James Atlas.

"Whatever the labor of any piece of writing, whatever its creative challenges and satisfactions, time had always taken me away from it," recalls V. S. Naipaul in *The Enigma of Arrival*, out this month from Knopf. "And, with time passing, I felt mocked by what I had already done; it seemed to belong to a time of vigor, now past for good. Emptiness, restlessness built up again; and it was necessary once more, out of my internal resources alone, to start on another book, to commit myself to that consuming process again."

From this process has come Naipaul's most self-revealing book, the chronicle of an inward journey that proved more harrowing than his travels in darkest Africa. *The Enigma of Arrival* marks a culmination in Naipaul's career; an autobiography in the form of a novel, it explains with ardor and eloquence what drove him to produce a body of work that makes him the rival of anyone writing in English.

Naipaul's books are fiercely candid, but he detests publicity and rarely sits for interviews. He's known to be proud, imperious, even rude. "His contempt is severe," notes Paul Theroux. His widely quoted opinion of the publishing scene: "an extraordinarily shoddy, dirty, dingy world" dominated by men with "the morality and the culture of barrow boys—street sellers, people pushing rotten apples." The people of his native Trinidad were "Monkeys," he once said, for whom "drumbeating is a higher activity." Every culture was primitive in its own way, even Oxford—"a very second-rate provincial university." On the way to see Naipaul, I remembered David Hare's portrait of Victor Mehta, the haughty Indian writer (based on Naipaul) in *A Map of the World*, whose books include a novel about journalists entitled *The Vermin Class*.

Naipaul's flat was on a quiet residential street of tidy red-brick apartments that had a newly renovated look. He led me down the hall past several sparsely furnished rooms and ushered me into the dining room. I asked if he had just moved in. "Yes, but I'm leaving," he said tersely. "The walls are too thin."

I wasn't surprised. Naipaul's characters are forever pulling up stakes, establishing themselves in seedy boardinghouses, then departing without a trace. Over the years, he has lived in India, Africa, South America, the Middle East. The Wiltshire village described so lovingly in his new book is the only permanent home he's ever had. Naipaul has lived there—first in a modest rented cottage, then in a house he bought and restored—for seventeen years.

Small, fastidious, precise in his gestures, Naipaul wears a plain gray sport coat and a blue tie. His hair is ebony black. Now fifty-four, he looks weary but fit; he's a vegetarian, drinks sparingly, does yogic exercises every morning. His features are delicate, austere; his expression is often pained.

In the dining room a woman, white-haired but with a handsome, youthful face—a character out of Iris Murdoch—brings us tea and slips away. It can only be Naipaul's wife, Patricia Hale, who for many years has closely edited his work. They met at Oxford and married in 1955. Yet no reader of Naipaul could presume him married; in twenty books, the only intimation of anyone else in the picture occurs in *An Area of Darkness*, where he refers—once—to his "companion." When he taught at Wesleyan, his wife remained in England. In the Wiltshire cottage, where he writes his books, he lives alone.

I ask him about *The Enigma of Arrival*. Why did he decide to write about England? "I've only been here thirty-six years," he says with a laugh. "It takes time to adjust." And why has he chosen to call the book a novel when it's so obviously autobiographical? "It has an autobiographical *crust*," he concedes, "but it's not an autobiography in the usual sense. It's impersonal. The man has no qualities of his own. He's anonymous, an observer. No detail of his own life ever intrudes."

Naipaul talks about himself with an eerie detachment: "One was lost in London." "One had no idea who one was." "One was alone." More than any other writer I know, he has invented himself, pieced together a coherent identity out of a multifarious past. Trinidad, where he was born in 1932, was "a dot on the map," he's often complained, "a ridiculous little island." A place—if you had ambition—to escape. "When I was in the fourth form," he recalled in *The Middle Passage*, "I wrote a vow on the end paper of my Kennedy's *Revised Latin Primer* to leave within five years. I left after six; and for many years afterwards in England, falling asleep in bedsitters with the electric fire on, I had been awakened by the nightmare that I was back in tropical Trinidad." Why nightmare? I ask.

"If you're from Trinidad, you want to get away," he says grimly. "You can't write if you're from the bush."

In 1950, Naipaul took up residence at Oxford on a government scholarship, but he's made no literary use of the experience (unlike just about every other writer who ever put in time there), and he's reluctant to discuss those years. "It was a difficult time," he says softly. "There was lack of money, uncertainty, great worry about my family. I was very isolated. My studies were of no importance. They didn't interest me." Hadn't there been some kind of emotional crisis at Oxford? "I had a mental disturbance owing to the strangeness of where I was, to loneliness. One was so far from home," he says. "So far from what one knew. It was an alien world, Oxford." He pauses. "It was clear one would remain a stranger."

It wasn't until he arrived in London at the age of twenty-one that his life as a writer began in earnest. "It was the most artificial thing for me to be a writer," he says now. "As a boy in Trinidad, I wanted to be a scientist, then a painter, but I couldn't buy a tube of paint." Installed at a desk in the typing room of the BBC, where he worked as a broadcaster for the Caribbean Service, he wrote a novel that was never published, began another, then a third. It was an arduous apprenticeship. "I was confined to a smaller world than I had ever known. I became my flat, my desk, my name." To have emerged out of Trinidad by way of India—his grandfather arrived from the province of Uttar Pradesh in the 1880s—was to have been doubly exiled from the start. To become a novelist in the stratified, class-conscious world of literary London was yet another form of exile. In a piece entitled "London" that appeared in the *T.L.S.* in 1958, Naipaul complained that he had written three books and made £300. "The Americans do not want me because I am too British. The public here do not want me because I am too foreign."

Still, three books—what strikes anyone is how precocious he was. Two of those books had appeared in print by the time he was twenty-six, they won prizes and got excellent reviews (from, among others, Kingsley Amis). By the time he published his masterpiece, *A House for Mr. Biswas,* he was an established writer in England, with a small but loyal following. He was a year shy of thirty. A triumph? Naipaul didn't see it that way. "I had dreamed of coming to England," he writes in *The Enigma of Arrival.* "But my life in England had been savorless, and much of it mean."

The main event of this novel-autobiography is a second nervous breakdown, suffered when Naipaul was in his late thirties, a "grief, too deep for tears or rage," brought on by the failure of a book. For two years he'd been working on a history of Trinidad (*The Loss of El Dorado*). In the midst of his research he resolved to leave England and go back to the New World. "The house I had bought and renovated in stages I sold; and my furniture and books and papers went to the warehouse." Four months later, a "calamity" occurred. The book was turned down; the publisher who'd commissioned it "wanted only a book for tourists." Naipaul was forced to return to England. Broke, exhausted, in need of a refuge, he retreated to a Wiltshire cottage on the grounds of a manor inhabited by a reclusive landlord, and it was there, "in that unlikely setting, in the ancient heart of England, a place where I was truly an alien, [that] I found I was given a second chance, a new life, richer and fuller than any I had had anywhere else."

These days Naipaul seems utterly at home in England. His clothes are tweedy, his shirts bespoke; his accent is unswervingly "U"; until a few years ago he ordered snuff from Fribourg & Treyer and dipped it with a silver spoon. He carries a British passport and thinks of himself as a British writer. (One publisher who made the mistake of advertising Naipaul as "a West Indian writer" was quickly dropped.) Yet he's often had bitter things to say about his adopted land. A decade ago he described England as "a country of second-rate people—bum politicians, scruffy writers and crooked aristocrats."

When I remind Naipaul of this observation, he questions me closely about my sources "I wouldn't make big remarks about England now," he says mildly. "It's a very humane place." What about the racism he encountered? The wrong word, I discover. "That is an eighties word," he says, slapping the table. "Don't oversimplify. We must not use anachronistic words." His dark, hooded eyes are bright with anger. "People come from all over; they have all kinds of roots. There's nothing strange about it. If you're an Eskimo, you want to define yourself." The humiliations he recalled with such agonized fervor in his work—the sense of excludedness, of marginality, that afflicts so many of his early characters transplanted from the West Indies to London—have given way to a sense of "racial pride." The crisis is over. England has become that green and pleasant land.

In *The Enigma of Arrival*, Naipaul surveys the gardens and valleys and farms of rural Wiltshire, the manor and its decaying grounds, the cottage where he writes his books, with a naturalist's penetrating eye. Beneath the picturesque surface, the shady lanes and meandering streams so beloved of urban exiles, is an aura of ominous change. In the course of the book, barbed-wire fences appear; the roads are paved over; buildings vanish overnight, leveled and replaced by new ones. Naipaul's Wiltshire is about as idyllic as Hardy's. No, he says, it wasn't the landscape that attracted him; it was community, his neighbors—the gardener, the servants in the manor house, the owner of the local car service. "One was dealing with people," he says with obvious feeling. "One was brought closer to others. They were available to one. It's the most benign place I've ever known."

A virtual recluse when he's working, Naipaul seldom answers letters from people he doesn't know, and insists that he hardly ever sees anyone. "I know fewer and fewer people," he says. Yet somehow when a name comes up—Theroux, Anthony Powell—it's someone Naipaul has talked to lately. "Very social people like Antonia Fraser, people who could lend him a cottage for the weekend—were onto him from the start," recalls the critic John Gross of Naipaul's early days in London. In New York, there are dinner parties given by his publisher at Lutece; there's the New York literary-dinner-party circuit. When he does go out, he goes out in style.

In the same way, he shrugs off references to his reputation. Routinely acknowledged as one of the pre-eminent writers of our day, frequently mentioned as a candidate for the Nobel Prize, he still maintains that he's largely ignored. "One never knows where one stands." He doesn't read the *Sunday Times*, not even when his own books are reviewed. Only once, in 1971, did he monitor the reception of a book he'd published. And what book was that? "I don't like to speak the names of my books," he says. Back in my room, I discover that it was *In a Free State*, for which he won England's prestigious Booker Prize, worth £12,000. Was he caught up in the speculation about its chances? For all his asceticism, Naipaul is keenly interested in money. "The capitalistic streak in him runs very deep," confirms one of his friends. He likes to know how much things cost. (He once asked a journalist if his wristwatch was a genuine Cartier.) He's reputed to be merciless in negotiating contracts. Last year, after he'd turned in *The Enigma of Arrival*, publishing circles in New York were full of talk about a proposal Naipaul's agent had circulated to several publishers for a new book, tentatively entitled *Slave States: A Journey Through the American South*. The asking price was said to be $300,000. Eventually, according to one source, there was a much lower offer. The project was shelved. "In the beginning, one was badly represented," he recalls. "I was a great believer in the adage that virtue would look after itself. Nowadays one is more clear-sighted." A few months ago, he stunned his London publisher, André Deutsch, by leaving for another house—Viking. Deutsch had handled Naipaul for twenty-nine years; he had published every one of Naipaul's books. "He never even thought it appropriate to send a postcard," says a bewildered Deutsch.

That is Naipaul: abrupt, easily slighted, wary of allegiances. "My vocation made me a free man," he declares. "I never had to stay in a job, never had to work for anybody. The peasant doesn't work for anyone else." He likes to say that he has no enemies, no rivals, no masters. "I fear no one." Perhaps not. But his books simmer with scarcely suppressed rage—the refugees gunned down on a barge in *A Bend in the River*, the rape-murder that ends *Guerrillas*. "Hate oppression; fear the oppressed," writes Naipaul's exiled Caribbean minister Ralph Singh in *The Mimic Men*. Once, on a visit to New York, he became so antagonistic about the people he saw on the street that a publisher cautioned him, "I wouldn't go around talking like that. You can get killed."

Yet he's capable of incredible tenderness and empathy. Think of the "Traveler's Prelude" to *An Area of Darkness*—to me the most powerful scene in all of Naipaul's work. It describes, in charged, hallucinatory prose, the night of a cruise ship's arrival at the dock in Alexandria, the passengers besieged by horse-drawn cabs jostling for a fare.

> Not far away, below a lamp standard stood a lone cab. It had been there since the late afternoon; it had withdrawn early from the turmoil around the terminal. It had had no fares, and there could be no fares for it now. The cab lamp burned low; the horse was eating grass from a shallow pile on the road. The driver, wrapped against the wind, was polishing the dully gleaming hood of his cab with a large rage. The polishing over, he dusted; then he gave the horse a brief, brisk rub down. Less than a minute later he was out of his cab again, polishing, dusting, brushing. He went in; he came out. His actions were compulsive. The animal chewed; his coat shone; the cab gleamed. And there were no fares.

The obscure, the expendable, the unmourned: these are the ones who haunt Naipaul. His books on India especially are chronicles of a nation he's likened to hell. What he saw there—men reduced to objects, men starving in the dust—appalled him. His critics have claimed that Naipaul is an enemy of the Third World, that he condescends to it. "The condescension is in those who don't notice," he responds. "You've got to be awfully liberal not to be moved by distress. When you see human degradation on that scale, you can never be the same again."

Reading Naipaul, you feel the powerful urgency that impels his talent. His genius is a genius lashed on by the sheer will to write. "One was so driven by ambition for so long," he says, "endlessly able to pick oneself up. There was always something over the hill." He writes his books in tremendous bursts of concentration. "I can't *be* with a book for more than thirteen or fourteen months," he says. "It's in one's head. You're absorbed with it all the living day. I've written each book as if it was the last book I was going to write." Writing for Naipaul is a desperate act; he once described the process as "a sickening." No, he replies sharply when I mention having read this; it's more a feeling of uncertainty. Does he still find writing difficult? "Not *difficult*," he snaps. "*Uncertain* is the word I used; full of stops and starts." But again and again he persists to the end, "fighting the Monkey side of my nature," as he once put it.

In the closing pages of *The Enigma of Arrival*, Naipaul recounts the sudden death of his younger sister and his journey back to Trinidad for her funeral. The book is dedicated to his brother, Shiva, who died eighteen months ago of a heart attack in London at the age of forty. If the new book is in some way more benign, less despairing than his others, it's still a book about death. Jack the gardener dies, Mr. Phillips the caretaker dies, the handyman murders his wife. The landscape itself begins to die, changed beyond recognition. What is the lesson of this book? "I know that we all die, that books date very, very quickly now," Naipaul says wearily, shielding his eyes. "The book culture is fading. Books are no longer important."

Naipaul's talk on this darkening afternoon is dominated by death. "I'm close to the end of creativity." "Death is very, very final." "I've put all my affairs in order." But isn't this simply the exhaustion of finishing a project? "Writing isn't a young man's game," he acknowledges. "It's for the mature, the suffering, the wounded—for people who need elucidation." He used to say he was old at thirty-four; at fifty-four, he has written more, seen more, lived more than most of his contemporaries. But he's still only middle-aged, I point out. He fixes me with his black, penetrating eyes. "I'm telling you how I feel." He hesitates. "There are no children . . . Perhaps that would have made it easier."

Our interview done, Naipaul is suddenly relaxed, affable, even gay. To my utter astonishment, I hear us talking about a subject so incongruous that I actually begin to blush. How much money do you need to live in New York? Naipaul interrogates me intently: $100,000? $150,000? $200,000? And how much does a journalist make? I laugh in disbelief and shrug. Do I own my apartment? he presses me. Does one hear people overhead? How much are co-ops going for these days? Under prompting, I offer a figure. He shakes his head: "Unbelievable."

Out on the street, walking among the twilight crowd, I glance back at Naipaul's window, a square of light in the dark, and think of the cabman alone on the dock.

An Elusive Master:
V. S. Naipaul Is Still Searching
Andrew Robinson / 1987

From *The Illustrated Weekly of India*, reprinted in *World Press Review* 34 (October 1987), 32–33. Reprinted here by permission of Andrew Robinson.

The works of the prize-winning writer V. S. Naipaul are grand in conception, unpretentious in style, and wonderfully varied in tone. His many novels and short stories include *The Mystic Masseur, A House for Mr. Biswas, Mr. Stone and the Knights Companion, The Mimic Men, In a Free State, A Bend in the River*, and now *The Enigma of Arrival*.

His nonfiction includes a history book, *The Loss of El Dorado*: a book on the Caribbean. *The Middle Passage*; *Among the Believers*; two books on India, *An Area of Darkness* and *India: A Wounded Civilization*; and a considerable body of journalism. In 1984 he published *Prologue to an Autobiography*, a probing of his background as a writer.

Naipaul was born in Trinidad in 1932, the eldest son of a small-time journalist and the grandson of an indentured laborer from northern India—facts that have haunted his entire life and his writing. For 18 years, until he made the unimaginable leap to Britain in 1950 on the back of an Oxford scholarship, Naipaul lived in the fold of Hindu orthodoxy among "neutered men, oppressed and cantankerous women, and uneducated children."

The compulsion to be a writer began there [he served at one time as *The Illustrated Weekly*'s London correspondent], but not the actual writing. The callow young Naipaul was to take many years to identify his true material. For him the Trinidad Indians were subjects fit only for embarrassment. Thirty-five years later he is still working to understand his particular, peculiar relationship to the mainstream of English literature.

At Oxford, "where I was said to be popular," Naipaul read English without much respect for the course and developed a great love of Shakespeare. He also brooded about his own conviction that he would write. In December, 1951, he "fell into a gloom" that lasted for 21 months.

A panic-stricken effort of will pulled him through. Since then, "I have felt I always have something to measure things against. Below all the ups and downs, the anxieties and tensions of living and writing, my life has been a celebration of the wholeness of the mind. I have enjoyed it enormously."

Naipaul's early novels and stories about Trinidad are all comic, with a wit that is mordant without being malicious. They were preparation for *A House for Mr. Biswas*, his novel about himself and his family (most of all, his father), which has a humor and pathos unmatched by postwar writing in English.

After the completion of *Mr. Biswas* in 1960, which took Naipaul close to his roots, he decided that he should also examine India at close quarters, instead of interpreting it through the distorting prism of his family. He spent a year there in 1962–63. The book that emerged, *An Area of Darkness*, offended many Indians with its unblinking focus on poverty and caste rigidity. "It's about me really, being an Indian immigrant in Trinidad," he says.

In the latest novel, *The Enigma of Arrival*, Naipaul's search for permanence, stability, and wholeness lies in Britain and in his relationship to rural Wiltshire, where he has spent, on and off, the past 20 years of his life. The writing is plainly autobiographical—in the first person. Naipaul comments, "The book has this autobiographical element, which I have long wanted to do, for a very simple reason. The neutral personality would not really be true enough."

You have said that Thomas Hardy's life may have been boring, but surely yours hasn't been?

My life has been extraordinarily dull. I think all writers' lives are boring because writers do nothing but work.

Are there any writers whose lives are not boring?

Their early lives tend to be rather interesting—and that is their capital. But it always breaks down with their first book. Nothing is as romantic in Dickens's life as that dropping of the first sketch by Boz into the mailbox.

Do you look on your childhood with regret that it wasn't happier?

No. I don't think like that. I think in another, more frightening way. There were so many abysses. What luck that one didn't just disappear.

Were you ever beaten in the way your characters often were as children?

I was never beaten at school. The boys made room for me because I was always the youngest person around. And that encouraged my wit. It was nice that this could happen in a multiracial society.

How did you take to the work in Oxford in the English course?
I liked the language side, the linguistic side. I think that unless one had been compelled at Oxford to give that great attention to Shakespeare, I would have missed his magic, which is a great love. One has to work at it.

Have the immigrants from Asia and the Caribbean changed British life?
I feel that there will be a lot of difficulty. I don't see how it can be avoided, especially with these immigrants who are not seeking a new identity or a new kind of citizenship. They are migrating to allow their barbarism to flower, so they can be more Islamic or more Sikhish than they can be in the comparative economic stagnation of their home societies. I think it is very dangerous.

What aspects of yourself do you feel to be specifically Indian?
The philosophical aspect—Hindu I would say. Speculative and probably also pessimistic. What I mean by pessimism is not things turning out badly, but a pessimistic view about existence; that men just end. It is the feeling that life is an illusion. I've entered it more and more as I've got older.

Do you expect to return to India to write?
No. To travel and to write is very hard—to assemble your notes, to do 200 miles in difficult weather, to have your wits about you when you're talking to people, and to remember what they have said.

You don't use a tape recorder?
No. I have always used a little notebook, which I write in later. With a tape recorder the conversation would not be concentrated. One would babble. One would not get the exercise of mind and memory that the need to write would give you. You would feel it's all there; there's no need for the mind to work at the material.

How has India changed in recent years?
India's development since I went there in 1962 has been extraordinary. The newspapers then were abominable. Reports of Parliament and speeches were like a clerk's writing. But after two generations there has been a great efflorescence of intellectual life. There is a publishing industry that did not exist in 1962. There is no problem that people are not talking about. There is great tolerance, and great human values, rather than rabble-rousing.

There seems to be an underlying feeling in your work that Western writers about India tend to be dishonest because they are themselves secure.

They are writing from their own point of view, with their own attitudes, which cannot be mine.

Are you still convinced that English cannot be a national language of creative power in India?

It could not be as grand as the Indian languages. A language has so many echoes—echoes of the epics, things you heard people say when you were a child, books you read at school. I do not see how Indians could use English with all these echoes and references that give density and taste and savor to a language.

Does America horrify you?
No.

Not even the manic Star Wars mentality?

No. Americans are really very nice, very humane people. What a humane civilization and culture to have been created from a big melting pot.

Wouldn't it be creatively interesting for you to live there some of the time?

I'd probably like to try. I have no plans, but it would be nice to be in a place where nearly everyone you meet is a stranger. As one gets older one does feel more of a stranger here. But this is not a profound or settled attitude of mine.

Going Back for a Turn in the East

Andrew Robinson / 1990

From *The Sunday Times*, 16 September 1990, 8, 14. Reprinted by permission of Andrew Robinson.

"The country's going from bad to worse," said the hotel manager in Bombay when V. S. Naipaul mentioned a vast street celebration he had just seen, by people formerly known as Untouchables. Naipaul strongly dissents, perhaps surprisingly for those who know his two earlier books on India. The third book, *India: A Million Mutinies Now,* is essentially an optimistic one.

"India's a good deal less shocking now," he says, "because there are so many places where you see movement . . . One opens the papers and things are being talked about and discussed. In 1962, when I first came, poverty was not talked about in India as poverty, people still spoke of poverty as romantic and poetic—a unique Indian gift to the world—holy poverty."

Naipaul and I last met three and a half years ago, when his complex, melancholy autobiographical novel *The Enigma of Arrival* was published. Then aged 55, he assured me that no more travel books could be expected from him. Why had he gone on to produce *A Turn in the South* (about the American south), and now India? He gave two reasons. The first was characteristically forthright. "I was physically tired of the act of writing, my wrists ached and my handwriting became illegible. I became very agitated about the way I would keep my journal, keep my notes." But then he came across a small electronic typewriter in a shop in New York. "It was like an answer to my prayers. It has altered my life; I was able to make my notes by hand and then work almost immediately on this wonderful instrument, and it didn't make any noise. It was a great excitement for me."

Then there was a second excitement he discovered, while in the American south, "how to travel in a new way." He emphasises the hard-won evolution of his travel writing from his first book, *The Middle Passage*, about Caribbean slavery. "When I undertook that in 1960, I was a little bit at sea. Of course I'd read the great European travel books . . . but how was a man from Trinidad to view the world? You go to a place you go to a hotel, but how do you move from there? You don't know what you want, but you almost know what you don't want. And as you move, the picture alters. What follows depends on what's gone before; you're making a whole, you're constructing something.''

In the south, Naipaul began to feel that the people he met could help in that construction more than he had permitted in the past. He would let them talk, keeping himself much more in the background. "And so in this book on India I thought it was better to let India be defined by the experience of the people, rather than writing one's personal reaction to one's feeling about being an Indian and going back.''

Some classic descriptive set-pieces apart, much of the latest book, therefore, consists of reported speech, shaped, of course, by the author. He begins in cosmopolitan Bombay and progresses in a roughly anti-clockwise arc, ending up in Kashmir, revisiting haunts. On the way we listen at length to a cross-section of Indian society: Muslim ghetto-dwellers, Hindu and Sikh communal leaders, slum-dwellers, middle-rank gangsters, retired and not-so-retired terrorists, back-to-basics brahmins, business executives, traders, politicians, scientists, writers, journalists, and former princes. By getting them to talk about the lives of their parents and grandparents, Naipaul deftly introduces a lively sense of history and gets far closer than any other writer to realising that elusive goal—a book that encompasses and penetrates both the contradictions and the unity of the subcontinent.

Naipaul is an extremely attentive listener, and a willing, witty, some-times scathing talker; but one feels that he dreads intimacy and cherishes solitary detachment. Paul Theroux, a friend since the mid-1960s, thinks India shows more "compassion" than the two books that preceded it. "I take care not to use the word," Naipaul comments, a faintly sardonic smile creasing his lips. "Compassion is a political word, isn't it?''

Rather than compassion, Naipaul has pity. He can never forget that he is the grandson of an indentured labourer who left eastern India for Trinidad just over a century ago—nobody knows exactly when. "I come from a people who were immemorially poor, immemorially without a voice. And because I feel that, I have a certain amount of regard for the political, democratic change that's happening to India. People who've not had a voice—ever—are slowly learning to exercise responsibility. It's a new thing—a very different thing.''

Listening to the people he meets reminds him of his father, who was the inspiration for Mr. Biswas of Naipaul's great novel, *A House For Mr. Biswas*, published in 1961. "I can easily make present again the anxiety of that time," Naipaul said of his twenties, "to have found no talent, to have written no book, to be null and unprotected in the busy world. It is that anxiety—the fear of destitution in all its forms, the vision of the abyss—that lies below the comedy of *A House For Mr. Biswas*."

Most of that comedy has disappeared from Naipaul's writing in later years, a fact that he regrets. He feels himself becoming more Hindu, closer to the idea of life being an illusion. "For many years I have sent myself to sleep with the idea of death—which is an aspect of this feeling that life is an illusion. Very violent pictures of death, I must say. I used to think of my head being cut off, with two strokes of an axe, rather than one . . . Nowadays I sleep with the idea of a bullet being put in the back of my head . . . it comforts me." ("Are you shocked?" Naipaul asked me a few days later, after his wife had expressed some concern about publishing this remark. I said I wasn't all that surprised, given his gloomy statements over the years.)

Pursuing his vocation over nearly 40 years has been anything but simple. It has often seemed an agony. "A lot of my work until, I would say, my second Indian book, was really snatched out of panic by a man who was really doubting his ability to go on. It's very hard to make novels out of experience so fractured and muddled. Novels, a body of work, come best out of whole and single societies."

India is an expression of Naipaul's admiration for the 19th-century novel. That fascinating century in India at last gains entry to Naipaul's canvas, giving better perspective to the events of our own century; in particular Gandhi's freedom movement and the independence of 1947. It is the same territory explored by Nirad C. Chaudhuri, Naipaul's only literary rival among commentators on India. Although Naipaul admired his first volume of autobiography, Chaudhuri's recent second volume, *Thy Hand, Great Anarch!* runs contrary to Naipaul's view, as his subtitle, *A Million Mutinies Now*, suggests. Both writers see empire as a basically reforming influence in India, but they differ over its long-term significance to Indian civilisation. Chaudhuri believes India has been going down the drain since the 1920s. "I cannot accept that," Naipaul says vehemently. "I cannot think that what was there before in the last century, or the previous century, was wonderful. My reading of it is that it was a dreadful mess, with most of the people unprotected. It was chaos. I see *now* as a great regenerative period in India."

In the last chapter he undertakes a return journey, to the place that bears for him the most intense of his memories of 1962—Kashmir. There we meet again the Muslim proprietor of the hotel Naipaul stayed in. He has prospered: the hotel is much bigger, he has made the pilgrimage to Mecca and his son is planning to be an accountant, and even to marry a foreign girl. It is a microcosm of progress in India, Naipaul implies, with

·"more people becoming less poor, more people taking control of their destinies," while all the time being held together, he claims by "a central will, a central intellect, a national idea: (the Indian Union) that did not exist before the British."

Less than a year after Naipaul was there, Kashmir was in flames. Some of the "million mutinies" had coalesced into a disastrous conflict, threatening the integrity of India. Should the centre hold it together by force? On the strength of Naipaul's book it is hard to predict: the best of those he met had some conviction, but the worst, including many of the politically powerful, are alarmingly full of passionate intensity.

The Unsparing Vision of V. S. Naipaul

Scott Winokur / 1991

From *Image*, Sunday, 5 May 1991, 8–15. Reprinted by permission of the *San Francisco Examiner*.

Dressed in white and garlanded with hibiscus flowers, reporter Seepersad Naipaul of the Trinidad *Guardian* brought the blade of a ceremonial cutlass down hard upon the neck of a sacrificial goat in a public ceremony on Friday, the 23rd of June, 1933. He placed the animal's severed head on a brass plate and presented it to the Hindu goddess, Kali.

Though it humiliated him, Naipaul had felt compelled to act after receiving an anonymous threat written in Hindi, the language of many Trinidad farmers. His offense had been to inform *Guardian* readers that the farmers were turning to the goddess—a grotesque figure associated with disease, death and destruction—rather than vaccinating their livestock against a form of rabies transmitted by vampire bats. He had used the phrases "superstitious remedies" and "amazing superstitious practices," and they had come back to haunt him.

Like the reporter, the farmers were descendants of indentured Indian laborers brought by the shipload to work in Caribbean sugar-cane fields some 50 years earlier. They had lived in lush West Indian and South American villages for generations now, but their faith and observances were those of the sun-baked Gangetic plain.

"Writer Kowtows to Kali to Escape Black Magic Death," the *New York Herald Tribune* reported in a dispatch from Port-of-Spain. "The writer was told he would develop poisoning tomorrow, die on Sunday and be buried on Monday . . . Today he yielded to the entreaty of friends and relatives and made the demanded sacrifice."

While the goddess had spared him, it was, in a sense, the beginning of the end for Seepersad Naipaul, a small, thin, delicate-looking man quietly aflame with literary ambition but fatefully restricted by the circumstances of life on a backward colonial island in a dim, drab time.

Unlike Salman Rushdie, a later Indian writer who also distanced himself under threat of death from heresy of his own making, Naipaul never recovered. He was destined to plod along for years in an obscure corner of the world, a psychologically damaged $80-a-month newspaper hack who read Dickens, Eliot and Conrad, scribbled occasional short stories and came away from it all empty-handed.

"He looked in the mirror one day and couldn't see himself. And he began to scream," his wife would say. By the age of 47, Seepersad Naipaul, the victim not only of ignorance and blighted hopes, but an unspecified nervous disorder and cardiac disease, was dead, quite literally from a broken heart.

Tragic as it was, Seepersad Naipaul's story wouldn't be noteworthy today if it weren't for the fact that this woebegone Indian fathered (perhaps as divine recompense) two sons who would cast off the encumbrances of home and culture and achieve what he had wished for himself, and vastly more.

The younger, Shiva, a novelist and a journalist, was perhaps best known to Northern Californians as the author of *Journey to Nowhere: A New World Tragedy*, an account of the self-destruction of San Francisco's demonic pastor, Jim Jones, and his People's Temple in Trinidad's neighbor republic, Guyana. Shiva has been dead six years; his heart also quit at an early age.

The elder, Vidiadhar Surajprasad, an Oxford-educated novelist and journalist who writes under the name V. S. Naipaul, has for some time been on the short list of candidates for the Nobel Prize in Literature; critics rank him among the greatest English writers of the 20th century, an author comparable to Joseph Conrad.

Naipaul, who is 58, has written 21 books, most of them centered on the theme of social and political displacement in post-colonial cultures. It is primarily on the strength of three that his place in literary history is assured: the early tragicomedy, *A House for Mr. Biswas*, and two astringent mid-career political novels about corruption and delusion in the Third World, *In a Free State* and *A Bend in the River*.

If his name is, nevertheless, only vaguely familiar, it may be because Naipaul's commercial success has been as small as his critical success has been large, and because he refuses to promote himself aggressively, believing it would be undignified.

He is content with his resulting lack of celebrity, noting with pride, that sales-conscious publishers are reluctant to sign him up ("They get a little glow from my reputation and that's really all") and that his core readership is very small: several hundred "shy, intelligent, quiet" people in this nation and at least one in England, presumably—Queen Elizabeth II, who knighted him last year.

A Nobel would widen this elite constituency. Generally favorable reaction to latest reportage—*India: A Million Mutinies Now*, portions of which he read recently before an appreciative audience in San Francisco as part of the City Arts & Lectures series—suggests the prize may be closer than ever.

He is being championed by critics of the first rank for the honor. "He has more stature than some of the people who have received it," says Roger Shattuck. And Alfred Kazin, another leading commentator, declares: "Before long he will get it. There are very few writers as gifted and as valuable. By force of circumstance and talent, he is truly unique."

If a day does indeed arrive when the gold Nobel medal comes to rest on V. S. Naipaul's chest, it would be a fitting end to a poignant intergenerational tale of aspiration, torment and attainment—a story of the Third World and the crushing nullity it can impose; of two intelligent men trying to break free of that constraint, and father failing, the son snatching from that failure the seeds of an enormous triumph.

"When I was about 6 or 7, he began to call me, to read to me. And I was dazzled. I found it beautiful. When he talked to me about writing, I decided to be a writer. I thought he knew—*we* knew—that was established," Naipaul said wistfully during a series of rare interviews here.

"His love was extremely important to me. It was a very curious kind of love. I felt responsible for him, even as a child.

"The circumstances of our colonial society didn't allow people to do too much, you know. So without understanding all this, I just saw his frailty.

"He always admired me. I knew that. I was aware that he thought I was somebody, even when I was small. That kind of love is a great thing, a great thing. It gives one an idea of oneself."

The man this child became has produced a body of writing as controversial, on a global scale, as Seepersad Naipaul's story about Kaliworship in Trinidad half a century ago.

For in novel after novel and travel book after travel book V. S. Naipaul insists upon being politically *in*correct, the contrarian, the conservative voice (a deep, resolute voice with the Oxbridge accent of the hated white man) stating emphatically what few dare to say: *That the demise of Western imperialism has not benefitted the peoples of Africa, Asia and Latin America nearly as much as some would like to believe.*

In one fashion or another, Naipaul is declaring, the mindless sacrifices to Kali continue.

The Third World he has written about for the last four decades is—in his dark, unblinking eyes—a festering sore, a realm of instinct and delusion controlled by corrupt leaders who prefer to lay blame for current misfortunes on accidents of history and long-gone colonizers, rather than to look inward and exercise what Naipaul calls "the gift of self-criticism."

"How people *need* the enemy," he says.

Writing in his new book about Sikh violence in the state of Punjab, an uprising motivated by the minority group's long-frustrated desire for religious independence, Naipaul observes: "Some of the good and poetic concepts of Sikhism were twisted. One such idea was the idea of *seva*, or service. When terror became an expression of faith, the idea . . . was altered. Now . . . terrorists lived only for murder . . . they lived hectically, going out to kill again and again. Every day there were seven or eight killings, most of them mere items in the official report printed two days later."

But Naipaul's contempt is not reserved for people of color only. Whites are targets as well, whether individuals or institutions: the "ugly" English dairyman in the autobiographical novel *Enigma of Arrival* ("a man who could give himself the best of reasons for doing strange things") . . . the publishing industry ("Publishers don't read the books—it's all done by mirrors") . . . the language of Rousseau and Flaubert ("French is now of no account, no consequence, a language spoken by some black people and some Arabs") . . . Connecticut's Wesleyan University, where Naipaul once taught ("inferior minds . . . an intolerable place").

Most hateful of all to him are white pseudo-intellectuals pretending to truly value Third World culture—men and women who, finding themselves beneath sub-Saharan skies, don dashikis, sip white wine, make it a point to extol the virtues of their suffering host countries, then slip home with steamer trunks full of precious artifacts. "Who more African than the young American who appeared among us, who more ready to put on African clothes and dance African dances?" he writes in *A Bend in the River* of a sometime Afrophile who flees to the States with crates of loot "no doubt to be the nucleus of the gallery of primitive art he often spoke of starting."

The sledgehammer drops noiselessly; Naipaul may rage, but his cool and unobtrusive writing style always achieves the "window" effect another political novelist, George Orwell, aimed for. "One needs clarity," says Naipaul.

Seeing clearly, probing, analyzing, getting what actually happens in society *absolutely right*—once this was every serious novelist's intent. Think of Austen, Zola, Dreiser. No more. The market has changed. Now readers in the West—fatigued by a century of relentless horror conveyed in picture, word and sound 24 hours a day—want tellers of wonderful tales, writers who believe literature's mission is to beguile, to provide a respite from the constant anguish of reality. And they have them in mystifiers such as Jorge Luis Borges, Gabriel Garcia Marquez and Isabel Allende.

Naipaul won't play this game; in fact, he despises it. There is too much that *needs* to be said, he insists.

The cultures of concern to him generally have lagged far behind the West; to the extent they have kept up, their adaptations often have been peculiar, even pathological. In the Third World's swirling mass of troubles he detects both vast societal problems and small disturbances of individual consciousness. He feels morally bound to discuss these things, virtually to the exclusion of all else.

Nor will he allow his cold-steel vision to be tempered by the normal human urge to comfort the oppressed. In *Among the Believers*, his nonfictional 1981 account of Islamic life in non-Arabic countries, he writes about a devout Muslim newspaperman in Karachi, Pakistan, who fantasized that he would have his articles anthologized, "like Art Buchwald," or, in the alternative, get a communications degree in the United States. "I had been aggressive with Nusrat," Naipaul wrote. "The assumption that—while Pakistan and the faith remained what they were, special and apart—the outside world was there to be exploited, had irritated me. I had said that he wasn't qualified to do what . . . he wanted to do . . . I told him . . . I didn't think his newspaper pieces would make a book."

Some might call this cruel, particularly in view of his own father's yearnings. But Naipaul believes his purpose is to disabuse; if hefty doses of vitriol are required to do the job properly, so be it.

"He is the supreme writer of disenchantment that we have now. Most Western writers grew up in a rationalized world hungry for enchantment, whereas he grew up in an enchanted world and was hungry for rationality. The targets of his contempt are almost always people who have some sort of delusion—he *hates* them," says Robert Hass, the UC-Berkeley poet and critic.

"He dislikes privileged people who are sentimental about primitivism in the Third World," Hass adds, "and he dislikes the posturing of Third World people whose only tactic is to blame their oppressor, and he is *pitiless* towards the fantasies of the helpless, which is what people don't like about him. But nobody makes more sense of what's gone on in the world at large than he does."

Robert Boyers of Skidmore College, editor of the quarterly *Salmagundi*, is one of the leading U.S. commentators on Naipaul. Boyers has met him once and spoken with him by phone several times. He is a great admirer. None of this seems to count with Naipaul, who has never been friendly. ("That's fine," Boyers says. "No reason why he needs to be friendly.")

According to Boyers, Naipaul fails only when he does not live up to the demands of his own "hard, unyielding intelligence." Boyers says this happens in his new book, *India: A Million Mutinies Now*, which is uncharacteristically generous toward individual Indians and unconvincing in its attempt to be hopeful about the overall situation in India today.

Naipaul's two previous books about his ancestors' homeland were sharply negative, but in the current volume he contends India is changing for the good: "With the development of an intellectual life in India, people are awakening to history. They're beginning to understand where they stand in the scheme of things. It's the beginning of a new way of looking at yourself."

Some critics have charged that false notes were struck and dubious claims were made because Naipaul is trying to win the Nobel Prize and believes softening his stance toward India improves his chances.

For his part, Naipaul has argued (disingenuously, one suspects) that *India: A Million Mutinies Now* is second in quality only to *A House for Mr. Biswas*. But he has admitted, too, that there have been occasions when he failed to perform up to his own standards, pointing to an early book about the Caribbean, *The Middle Passage*.

While researching that book, he discovered a "messianic" side to Caribbean politics, rooted, he thought, in the fantasy life of West Africans—an inner world of religion, magic and pure feeling. "There was a fantasy that the real world began at night, that people's roles were reversed and white men became phantoms."

Though he has no religious feelings of his own, he was sympathetic to this collective mental exercise: "It was one way African people were able to preserve their souls." But the daytime consequences of such fervor were harmful, he decided; reality required other modes of thought.

When it came out, the book didn't adequately reflect his doubts—it simply wasn't as tough-minded as it should have been, he thinks now. "It's too romantic about Negro racial politics, about the idea of racial redemption. I should have expressed what I really felt deep down: *that racial politics were going to destroy those islands*. All those places are going to be Haiti in the end, and those who can are going to get away with green cards and come to America and talk about revolution. The book should have insisted on people being more rigorous and not indulging in sentimentality or wallowing in self-pity. It should have stated that that was dangerous, a dead end, that it was going to lead to self-forgiveness."

To Naipaul, self-forgiveness amounts to telling oneself it's all right to be sick. Some things in the Third World should *not* be forgiven, he believes. They should be diagnosed and cured, like an illness.

"It's really wonderful that we no longer laugh at people with disabilities in Trinidad," he said, by way of example. "Black people once laughed at people's disabilities. It was very cruel. I remember the black audience at the Port-of-Spain cinema when the concentration camps were uncovered in Germany at the end of the war. The black audience, you know, *shocking me* by laughing at the inmates in the newsreels. I remember, too, black people in the Caribbean laughing at pictures of Africans in the cinema.

"These things have to be understood, not hidden away. I suppose it goes back to human weakness, human frailty, human incompleteness— back to the rivalry in the days of slavery between the newly arrived and the ones already there, between the Creole slaves and the 'new Negroes,' as they were called.

"I wish we could forget it. Probably many people *would* forget it. It's a shocking thing to remember, but I'm just recording the kind of cruelties one deals with. One doesn't want to wound people. But, you know, it was a *disturbing* thing."

Twenty years later, he took pains to overlook nothing, to forget nothing and to forgive nothing when he set his sights on a large portion of the Nation of Islam, traveling for months in Iran, Pakistan, Malaysia and Indonesia in an effort to understand what he called Muslim "rage" and "hysteria." The result, *Among the Believers*, depicted a religion described by Naipaul as one of "fear and reward, oddly compounded with war and worldly grief."

For the Western reader perplexed by the mass psychology of Middle Eastern and Asian peoples, the book was an illumination, but a frightening one. "The faith was pushing men to extremes . . . No one could ever be sure that he was good enough as a Muslim . . . Men . . . made greater and greater demands on themselves . . . The world was full of traps . . ."

Except for the Koran and received tradition, Naipaul contended, Muslims deliberately navigated the modern world without a compass, publicly rejecting the offerings of a Western society perceived as sinful and menacing, while privately trying to exploit that same society's abundant educational and technological resources. The culture forced people to be two-faced, he felt. "It made for a general nervousness. It made people hide from the visitor for fear that they might be betrayed," he wrote of Malaysia in particular.

Reporters turned to Naipaul this winter when they wanted a leading cultural figure to make sense of Saddam Hussein. Naipaul testily reminded them that he'd written about an Arabic faith as practiced by non-Arabs and sent them packing.

Finally, at the urging of New York's Manhattan Institute, he gave an address, later published in *The New York Review of Books*. "I was to discover that no colonization had been so thorough as the colonization that had come with the Arab faith that everything before the faith was wrong, misguided, heretical . . . The faith abolished the past. And when the past was abolished like this, more than an idea of history suffered. Human behavior, and ideals of good behavior, could suffer . . ."

All this bashing has made Naipaul an object of unmitigated scorn for some writers of African and Asian descent. "Ask him," advised one prominent minority writer, "why he hates the color of his skin so much." An Asian author, playing up the title *India: A Wounded Civilization*, an earlier effort by Naipaul to fathom his ancestral culture, remarked bitterly: "It's not India that's wounded—it's *his* psyche. *I'm* not thinking every second about the color of my skin."

Driven to discover and perhaps trumpet what is good in their own heritages, Naipaul's critics find it hard to understand why a man as experienced and talented as he focuses on what is bad and treats it as if it were immutable, a death sentence of sorts. "Professional pessimism," West Indian poet and playwright Derek Walcott called it.

Writers such as the Antigua-born novelist Jamaica Kincaid and African American authors Al Young and Ishmael Reed see Naipaul as an enormously gifted moral failure: a man of color trying to pass for white, trying to pose as a member of the English upper class, to mimic the oppressor's arrogance.

"He just annoys me *so* much, all my thoughts are intemperate and violent," Kincaid said. "I think probably the only people who'll say good things about him are Western people, right-wing people. I don't want to way 'white.' "

Reed, grouping Naipaul with two other against-the-grain minority writers, Shelby Steele and Salman Rushdie, contended his audience was "the white insecurities market," intellectuals and academics seeking confirmation of "fears and superstitions" about the dark-skinned "Other" and "a sort of Kiplingesque reassurance that the West is best."

And this, Reed said, was a last, desperate attempt by white liberals to stem the surging tide of multiculturalism. "These guys should manage to make all the money they can now because they're playing to the same market Reagan played to, the morning-in-America market," he said.

Others, no less critical, are more respectful of Naipaul's achievements.

Native Indian C. J. Wallia is a writer and editor who studied at Stanford and now teaches at Berkeley's Vista College. Wallia, who has read virtually everything Naipaul has written, may be a perfect example of the "intelligent, quiet" person whose loyalty the author claims. Yet Wallia is angry at Naipaul today; he feels betrayed by the latest book, *India: A Million Mutinies Now.* "It's understandable that the Queen knighted him last year—he's England's favorite 19th-century Englishman!" declared Wallia, who is half Hindu and half Sikh. He calls the book an apology for British imperialism and a virtual libel against Sikhs, who represent about 2 percent of India's population of 880 million. "The Sikhs have been fighting almost 40 years now to establish a separate homeland, similar to the state of Israel, but he blames them for the problem, not the majority. It's another example of his blaming the victim in reference to India."

Bharati Mukherjee, an Indian American novelist at UC-Berkeley, has been reading Naipaul since her student days. Her reaction to his work and to his quarrelsome personality is complex. She thinks he is a likely Nobelist. But she also pities the man, in a sense, though she herself might not call it that.

Mukherjee, the Swiss-educated daughter of a wealthy Bengali manufacturer, has spent time with Naipaul, interviewing him years ago for *Salmagundi* and socializing with him while he was in San Francisco. He has been both cordial and insulting to her, and she has criticized his work. To Mukherjee, Naipaul is a mass of defenses, a personality in knots, obsessed with his own expatriation, with his in-bred cultural distance from what is, for him, the center of the universe: London.

To obscure this fact, Mukherjee believes he tries to be an Englishman's Englishman: icy, aloof, superior, a model of European intellect. It's a tense, difficult job, especially if your skin is chocolate and your hair midnight black. He *must* believe these things to be true, and prove as much to himself again and again, or it all threatens to fall apart.

"He travels to confirm his Eurocentric prejudices," Mukherjee said, crediting the remark to the director of the University of Iowa's International Writing Program. "While the shepherd in England is to him a noble person, the water carrier in a Third World country is a buffoon.

"There is great psychological and attitudinal divide between a colonial and a post-colonial. So that even though age differences might not be that of a whole generation—I was born in 1940—his take on situations is very different from mine," she explained, speaking perhaps not only for herself but for many educated people from non-white backgrounds in North America and England today.

"He was brought up as a minority in a race-conscious society, whereas

I was brought up as part of the mainstream. Our sense of self and our attitudes are naturally different. He is exploring expatriation, which implies a distancing from the subject. Irony is his natural tool. While I have moved from that kind of mordant and self-protective irony, I have put down roots. I'm writing with affection and sympathy."

To critics such as these, Naipaul replies: "I have nothing to say. I would find it impertinent to talk about individuals who are colleagues in the writing business."

But others are eager to speak for him. Robert Boyers argues that Naipaul is perfectly justified in sounding like the ruddiest-cheeked Englishman who ever penned a word for publication, if that's what he chooses. "He identifies with white, Western intellectuals and *he has every right to do that*. There's no reason why a person of color *needs* to be writing out of a perspective associated with the Third World, why he should be *expected* to manifest solidarity with the group from which he issues. There's something grotesque about demanding of a world-class writer that he hew to a party line or an ethnic perspective. He's been very frankly associated with Western values and he's used *that* perspective to criticize what's happening in the Third World—quite justifiably, some of us would say."

Naipaul, who has been everywhere, had never seen a redwood tree, so I took him to Muir Woods one damp and foggy morning, the idea being to introduce a monument to a monument and see what came of it.

I suspected that he was really two men: an extremely self-conscious English literary colossus who just might be the equal of another cultural transplant, the Polish-born Conrad, and a rambunctious little man with all the usual impulses, appetites and enthusiasms—relatively undiminished, too, despite his years. I was hoping the second would emerge beneath the awesome 200-foot-tall trees, so disarming when beheld the first time.

As a public figure, he can be very hard on people, journalists especially; he sees very few, and those he does grant an audience had better be punctual, familiar with *all* 21 of his titles and original in their questioning. It's necessary for the interviewer to prove worthy of the subject, in other words, or the subject, Naipaul, may find a way to make life briefly miserable for the interviewer.

But people who have been with the writer when his professional guard is down speak of a somewhat different person: a man of intense, free-ranging curiosity; a playful, amusing, bitchy, unfailingly clever man; a man with an impressive memory and wonderful powers of observation; a lover of good food and fine wine who is at the same time preoccupied by his own physiological processes, digestive and otherwise (a carry-over, probably, from his asthmatic childhood).

In short, the closer one was allowed to look, the more colorful—and peculiar—this private, controlling personality became.

For example, it is strange to think of one of the world's leading authors agonizing over hosiery in a department store. But Naipaul did exactly that while he was in San Francisco, spending 45 minutes in Macy's on Union Square trying to decide whether he should purchase dark-blue socks that were 80 percent cotton or 92 percent cotton. His skin, it seems, is very sensitive.

The City got him thinking about AIDS, too, and he wondered if he could contract the virus in an upper Market Street restaurant. He was assured he couldn't. He turned his attention to diners at a table across the way. "Aren't those the ugliest people you've every seen? Don't you think they were put there to punish us?" he asked his companion.

Naipaul's own interests appear to be strictly heterosexual, though some critics say his writing—a sodomy scene in his novel *Guerrillas* is often cited—suggests he is a misogynist. He has been married to the same woman for 36 years. "What does she do?" he was asked. "She does nothing, nothing at all!" he replied, laughing, as if the question were ridiculous. But later he admitted that he leaned heavily on his wife, reading to her each day's literary output. Reliable sources say there is a second woman, stashed somewhere in the United States. "He's an old-fashioned man," one commented.

Naipaul grabbed his hat, his sneakers and his asthma medicine and we set off for Muir Woods. He said that he makes the trip from his South Kensington flat to his country home in Salisbury in 90 minutes, driving 80–85 miles an hour in his Saab. (The flat, decorated with Daumiers and 17th century pieces from Rajasthan, is too noisy for work, so he writes in the country.) "My car doesn't like to go 95 miles an hour," he said with disappointment.

Muir Woods stunned him.

"Yes! Yes!" he cried. "Amazing! Yes! Yes!"

He tilted his head backward to see the forest canopy, plunged his hands into his pockets and whirled around, the hem of his coat flying outward, like a skirt.

"Yes! Yes! Yes!"

For several minutes he was speechless. Then he said Muir Woods must be a perfect place for meditation. After that, he was filled with questions about the height and age of the fog-shrouded trees.

"In India," he said, "they would cut all these down. Indians don't like trees."

As we walked along, a sweet smell wafted up from creekside. Naipaul sniffed the moist air. A leaf was plucked from a tree, torn to pieces and held under his nose. The smell, bay, was lovely.

We walked farther. Suddenly he stopped, plunged his hands back into his coat pockets and spun on his heel again.

"A snake!" he whispered. "I smell a snake!" But there was no noticeable smell and nothing could be seen.

Naipaul sniffed the air again. He was sure of it. He'd learned to detect reptilian scents in Trinidad, where "serious" snakes lie in wait for small boys. "They smell like fish, you know. All of them, however small."

Naipaul's own childhood was miserable. Much of the time his immediate family lived in crowded conditions with his mother's clan, a large Hindu family composed, he writes, of "neutered men, oppressed and cantankerous women, uneducated children." His bookish father—the struggling writer who slept beneath a picture of O. Henry and used a desk made of packing crates—was a second-class citizen in the extended family and not particularly compatible with his mother.

Naipaul felt bored, tense and generally disturbed. Every three weeks he suffered an asthma attack, which went untreated because no doctor on Trinidad was equipped to give him a shot of adrenaline.

"The older I grew, the more I saw what a wretched childhood it was. I thought it was all right then, not so bad. But that is nature's way of concealing certain things from people. You know, children are rather *dumb* creatures. But I had a disturbed, disturbed childhood. One felt unsettled. One lived at the margin, the edge. The world was stopped, was not real, in fact, for me. It was the nature of my life. These are enormous feelings."

From them there would emerge a sense that the world was decaying, that he had been born into a world past its peak. "I had always lived with this idea. It was like my curse," he says in *Enigma of Arrival*. "It was an Indian feeling," he explained here. "I think that thing about 'past the peak' has to do with the original migration."

Closely associated was another unpleasant feeling, the sense that the objects of everyday life, from the rusted staples in a book published in India to the clothing on his back, were inferior by design, as if to do things well—to strive for excellence in *anything* in the material world, really—were an offense to Hindu morality. "It's forgetting yourself. Like trying to be too clean, too fussy, too particular. It's challenging God, really. You are touching on something very important. Yes. One grew up

feeling that very *strongly*. Yes." But this he would shed easily in later
years, becoming a perfectionist, demanding a great deal of himself and
others.

Ancient India also asserted itself in relations with other islanders—
Africans, Asians and Anglos. Indians intentionally stood apart. Here past
appears to have been prologue. Any claims Naipaul makes today about
the deficiencies of specific cultures—no matter how well-reasoned they
may seem to be—probably should be considered in light of remarks such
as these:

"I'm going back into deep realms. First of all, you must know that
Indians have always lived with the idea of groups, people belonging to
different groups, always. Different caste groups, different religious
groups. You live with the idea of the world outside and the world inside.
You live inside your own group, and once you're inside, life is inviolate,
you never think about the outside. When I returned to my grandmother's
house in the country and that gate was closed, it was another world. We
lived in our shut-in world.

"What I'm saying, too, is that you have this idea of other, The Other.
You don't actually see them completely, you know. These are the caste
things one grew up with. It was part of the instinctive life of an old,
ritualistic Asian culture. It was just what is. It was very much part of my
way of thinking and feeling."

School was his sole outlet. He could "press a little switch" and step
into a better, brighter world there. "I was the smallest boy and rather
young. To my great surprise, I was good. I was quite shocked when I
became head of the class." Buoyed up, he began to entertain ideas that
he was physically attractive, as well. He would gaze at his arms and legs.
"I thought I was very . . . very *nice*."

But the modicum of self-esteem evaporated when he was 13 or 14.
Boys in his class were discussing good looks. "No one mentioned the
fact that I could even be considered. It was a great, great shock to me. It
worried me. It worries me to this day. I was losing something important.
Never recovered. It became very acute at Oxford because, you know, at
that age one is sexually very charged. I felt disadvantaged."

Sent to England on a Trinidad government scholarship in 1950 to study
literature, Naipaul never again would see his father or hear the man's
voice. "There was no telephone. It was like going away in the ancient
world. You went away forever."

At Oxford he continued to suffer. "I drifted into something like a
mental illness," he would write. The work was unpleasant and the women
beyond reach. Coming from a culture in which marriages were arranged,

he lacked all the graces. He waited, nonetheless, for an initiation: the moment he would become a writer. "The wish to write came first, and then you began to look for the material." There would be some sort of mystical transformation, he felt, a ring of creative fire through which he would pass in a spasm of mind and spirit, as if all his previous life had been prolonged gestation.

Yet months and years passed without the blessed event occurring. "I was waiting for some kind of intellectual miracle. The miracle didn't occur at Oxford." He couldn't find his voice; his material eluded him. He wrote only what was required by his tutors.

At 23 he left Oxford for London filled with fear, a dread inherited from his father. "With the vocation, he . . . transmitted to me . . . his fear of extinction . . . which could be combated only by the exercise of the vocation," Naipaul writes. "And it was that fear, a panic about failing to be what I should be, rather than simple ambition, that was with me when I came down from Oxford in 1954 and began trying to write . . ."

The breakthrough came 10 months later when he managed to get on paper his first publishable sentence. Then, in rapid succession, he produced three novels about the Caribbean, *The Mystic Masseur*, *The Suffrage of Elvira* and *Miguel Street*. "To become a writer, that noble thing, I had thought it necessary to leave," he writes. "Actually . . . it was necessary to go back. It was the beginning of self-knowledge."

A pattern would be set: he wrote (by hand, usually, often without changing from his pajamas); edited himself severely, allowing little or no tinkering by others; his book came out after he found a publisher who didn't consider his material too alien; he was praised by critics but drew the attention of few readers; and he began anxiously to seek ideas and material for his next project, never sure they would materialize.

The transformation had occurred—he had redeemed his father's life and raised his own to the level of his dreams—but he was still marginal, still doomed to suffer. Genius had to be its own reward: his first three books won two prizes but earned less than $1,000, total. "The Americans do not want me because I am too British. The public here do not want me because I am too foreign," he told *Times Literary Supplement* in 1958.

His best book would be his fourth, *A House for Mr. Biswas*, a rich, inspired story of a little man seeking a place for himself in the world, a man very much like his father. Robert Haas calls *Biswas* "more psychologically accurate and painful than any Dickens novel" and compares Naipaul to Chekhov in his ability to portray his subjects with unsentimental accuracy.

Naipaul remembered the personal drama behind *Biswas*: "It took seven to eight months to get it started. I knew I was writing a very big book. If my father was alive, clearly, I wouldn't have been able to write it. I wouldn't have wanted to do it. I probably wouldn't have even seen the material, the way you don't see things in front of your face. Do you understand? My talent wouldn't have been stretched at that early stage by this literary labor. You have the talent, but you have to *develop* it. I don't know whether his death wasn't a kind of creative liberation for me. No one was looking over my shoulder."

Biswas was followed by seven novels, the last, *A Bend in the River*, appearing in 1979, if *Enigma of Arrival*, a strange, difficult autobiographical fiction published in 1987, is excluded. *In a Free State*, an experimental novel about British expatriates in a strife-torn African nation, won England's prestigious Booker Prize in 1971.

The first book that got significant attention in the United States was *Guerrillas*, a 1975 novel about murder and revolution in the Caribbean. "It was written with great excitement," Naipaul said. That may explain its success in this nation—and its weakness as a novel.

"I can see why people reading *Guerrillas* might think he was a racist. There's certainly an argument to be made for its being a tremendously *reactionary* book. It's also misogynist," Hass said. "Naipaul takes this black character and visits on him all of his own self-loathing as a colonial. The black revolutionary writer has a white upper-class groupie-journalist girlfriend. He rapes her in the beginning of the book and sodomizes and kills her at the end of it. It's a book about the two kinds of people he hates most, posturing Third World revolutionaries and adoring white liberals. In my view it's his worst, most repellant book. But it was the one that won the hearts of American reviewers—it made his literary reputation here."

Four years later, Naipaul published *A Bend in the River*, a novel about an East African from an Indian merchant family trying to run a hardware business in a land gripped by tribal violence, political turmoil and Western exploitation. Boyers calls *A Bend in the River* one of the century's great political novels.

The last decade has been given over chiefly to journalism about the Third World, the American South and his own past—"books of inquiry and exploration" Naipaul calls them.

At its best, such as *The Return of Eva Perón* (with *The Killings in Trinidad*), Naipaul's reportage is so focused and precise that it's difficult to imagine the material being handled in any other way. Whether talking to Baptists in Mississippi, Indians in Venezuela or Muslims in Bombay, he said, his goal always is to "understand the other man." This doesn't necessarily result in praise or even sympathy. It results in clarity, all he cares about.

"I meet people. I talk to them. I ask people to introduce me to people they know. And I go in a jacket—a lightweight dark-blue silk jacket on the India book. The jacket is always important because it has the notebooks, two small notebooks that can disappear in my pocket. I never tape-record. The point of the notebook is that it wouldn't upset the man who has not been interviewed before. I take down his words, to his dictation.

"It's a distinct method because it's a writer's appreciation of speech, the novelist's way of looking. And a little bit of the historian's view. So many things come into play while I'm shaping this inquiry. I don't have a series of questions, but my questions become very pointed because so much work has been done in my mind before. It's an *encounter*, a free-wheeling inquiry."

He filled 15 notebooks working 15-hour days seven days a week for five months while researching the 520-page India book. At night he pored over his notes and organized his narrative on an electronic typewriter. "You're operating on about three different levels. It's very exciting. It's not strictly journalism because in the end it takes too long—five months of travel and nine months of writing. I compose by hand."

The project exhausted him; he was interrupted continually by asthma attacks triggered by the noxious fumes of Indian-made cars.

He said he intended to go on—essays here and there and another book about the Caribbean. "My only wish is to work. I do *nothing* when I'm not working on a book. I do *nothing*." But he gave the impression of a man for whom the possibility of depletion is very real.

"You know, it's been such a long career now. I've done an *immense* amount of work. One has written in different ways at different times. It's a great *achievement* we're talking about, a great intellectual labor over many, many years. It's very *hard* to write about the mixing of continents. A great effort, a great effort. The books are varied, and the inquiry expands, and the vision expands, and the knowledge expands."

He said all this not with pride or self-importance, but with a tired, quiet, almost clinical detachment—seeing clearly, letting the truth, as he knows it, have its way.

Stranger in Fiction

Andrew Robinson / 1992

From *The Independent on Sunday*, 16 August 1992, 23. Reprinted by permission of Andrew Robinson.

"I'll tell you the way I try to write. If you look at anything very honestly, without prejudices—prejudices either of hope or a political point of view—many things are contained in what you observe. But you . . . can only say I saw what I saw—and try to look at that."

V. S. Naipaul is speaking about the Republican Party Convention in Dallas in 1984, which he attended and wrote about, side-stepping the clichés and received ideas of American election journalism. But he has applied the principle in almost all his published work. This now runs to 10 books of non-fiction and 11 of fiction (and a further book well under way) with settings as far apart as Trinidad and the Caribbean, Argentina, the American South, England, central Africa, India, and the Islamic world as far afield as Indonesia. None of them is less than good; many are outstanding; and more than one is great. He has won literary prizes, been awarded honorary doctorates from Oxford and Cambridge, and was made a knight in 1990 (though he does not call himself "Sir"). He is perhaps the most wide-ranging and penetrating writer in English today.

Tomorrow he will be 60. He was born Vidiadhar Surajprasad in Trinidad, which was in 1932 just an insignificant pink dot on the map of empire. His father, a journalist on the *Trinidad Guardian* and an independent-minded man, died in debt when his son was just 21, away studying English at Oxford on a government scholarship. The family, who were orthodox Hindus, came from Eastern India; one of Naipaul's grandfathers was an indentured labourer, part of the great diaspora of Indians in the nineteenth century who settled wherever the British developed rubber, tea and sugar plantations.

Empires—past and present—fascinate Naipaul; imperial themes bind his work into a whole. But unlike most colonial migrants to Britain, he is not partisan. In book after book he has articulated the pain of colonial and post-colonial life with empathy and often comedy; but his impatience with Third World special pleading has not softened with success. He recalls that he was "utterly destitute," when he came down from Oxford in 1954. No one would give him a job.

"I think it was for racial reasons," he says evenly, when asked why. "But I've never worried about it. I no longer think about it—maybe because of living here in this valley." We are sitting in the Wiltshire cottage where he lives with his wife Patricia whom he met at Oxford. Prodded, he becomes vehement, his face creasing into a grimace.

"I think it's wrong to think about it. When you consider the racial politics of Trinidad and Guyana and the Caribbean islands; when you consider the excesses that have been committed in the racial riots between Africans and Asians; when you consider the massive 'ethnic cleansing' that accompanied the creation of Pakistan—you feel that no one should come to here and speak about racial prejudice. People should hold their peace. Because to do otherwise is to expect a higher standard of behaviour from other people than you expect from yourself."

"Ethnic cleansing": a 1992 phrase for ancient conflict. Naipaul's interest in military history, and extensive travels in places where there is strife between peoples, lend weight to his analysis. "What's happening in Yugoslavia is dreadful, but I would like to ask: is this what happened in the Turkish empire? Is this how the Turks kept their empire, keeping all these ethnic groups at dangers drawn for four centuries? Are they to some extent responsible? I am wondering about their despotic rule: their empire vanished and left nothing behind *except* disregard—unlike other more creative empires, like the Romans, and the British empire and the French."

He is against Western military intervention: "So many people will get killed whose war it isn't. I think the Turks should be asked to intervene militarily; it's their problem, they should take the refugees. It's part of their old empire, they made these people Muhammadan. They should take this over, send some of their dreadful soldiers there, who made such a messy invasion of Cyprus."

Naipaul is almost equally severe on the United States for its role in Afghanistan. "When you start playing geo-politics, and you have your big cause to defend, you get so morally twisted that you become responsible for certain messes in the world. You support the Afghans fighting their brave wars against the Russians, you represent them as freedom fighters, and then what happens? You've got fundamentalists and others killing one another in Kabul, and a spot of ethnic cleansing going on there. Who's responsible for that, at the end of the day? Who gave them the arms? America should accept its responsibility and admit: 'We cracked these barbarians up to be freedom fighters'. But the Americans say 'No, no! We don't think we'll do anything about them now.' "

Intellectual corruption bothers Naipaul. It offends his conviction that writing is a "nobel vocation." The writer must attempt to perceive and define the truth, however unpalatable: "The past for me—as colonial and writer—was full of shame and mortifications. Yet as a writer I could train myself to face them. Indeed, they became my subjects." For Naipaul, the compelling aspect of communism, and now its collapse, has been its impact on the West. He was never interested in writing about the Soviet Union; he felt he had seen similar tyranny too often in Asia and Africa and the Caribbean.

"You had the people's revolution, the people's triumph, and then you had all these dreadful men who lived off the fruits of it." The "pretend Marxists" in Western universities, especially in the US, enraged him: "Marxism became a posture in the 1980s, which enabled very stupid people to pretend they had a coherent view of the world."

Naipaul undoubtedly likes to needle people he considers narrow-minded but he has a strong and deep-rooted sympathy for the poor. Thirty years after his journalist father died in debt, Naipaul wrote: "I can easily make present to myself again the anxiety of that time: to have found no talent, to have written no book, to be null and unprotected in the busy world." When in 1961 he published a book about his father, his great comic novel, *A House for Mr. Biswas*, that anxiety—"the fear of destitution in all its forms, the vision of the abyss"—lay below the comedy.

Houses are important to Naipaul in his work and his life. The search for a house in Trinidad holds together *Mr. Biswas*; the decay of an Edwardian manor house in Wiltshire, in the grounds of which Naipaul lived for more than a decade from 1970, holds together his most recent novel, the intricate *The Enigma of Arrival*. For the last 10 years he and his wife have owned a turn-of-the-century cottage near Salisbury. Before that Naipaul rented and owned flats and houses in London, some of which have found their way into his novels, too. He was not satisfied with any of them.

But one feels Naipaul has not got his heart in bricks and mortar and English rural life. He has no wish to pose as a country gentleman. He loves the solitude, the long thoughtful walks, the nearby barrows and *Turmuli*, the fruit trees he has planted in his garden. But he feels himself a stranger, in a way that he tries acutely to define in *The Enigma*. Reviewing it, Bernard Levin called Naipaul an "inquiline": That is, a lodger, and also an animal that lives in another's nest. Naipaul likes the word.

"When I see the sun set—here at Stonehenge—there is a way that it is somebody else's sun, somebody else's landscape, it has somebody else's history connected with it. I can't avoid that: that's the way I think." And the place gets more, no less, mysterious as he gets older: "the way things should. It would be awful if you just stopped reacting, if your knowledge of places stopped. The idea of human beings and their destinies should get more miraculous and odd."

Occasionally, visiting Salisbury by bus from the village, he calls at St. Thomas's Church near the cathedral to see the largest Domesday painting in England, dated 1475. The naked medieval figures, in heaven on the left, in hell on the right, "men naked, beyond their control, the wings of the consoling angels as fearful and unnatural as the bird or reptile swallowing the damned," appeal to him.

Recently he has been dipping into the Bible again (as well as into Cicero, Darwin, Balzac, and CLR James). He uses the New English version, not the Authorised. "I can't bear the Authorised. It has been a source of corruption. It has given people an idea of beautiful language which is entirely theatrical and wrong and antiquated. . . . Those tribal chronicles . . . can stand purity and clarity of language, they don't need 'doths' and 'even untos'; they don't need these distractions, they don't need the rhythms of speech that dull you," says Naipaul emphatically.

His new book is not a novel, nor is it conventional autobiography, though it draws on his peripatetic experience. "It's a series of narrations. People occur in one place, then occur elsewhere in the course of your life. People you knew in Trinidad as a child turn up in London and then you see them as big men in Africa, then you see them as criminals making money somewhere else. One had to find a form for that. I hope it will be very light."

"In a sense he has extended the range of the novel" says Naipaul's former tutor at Oxford, Peter Bayley. "He's a most distinguished writer, and a complex man of very great charm, fascination, intelligence and distinction. I would use the word 'lovable'."

But love is precisely the emotion some—Salman Rushdie included—cannot find in Naipaul. Where, they ask, is the love? Where is the compassion? " 'Compassion' is a political word, isn't it?" Naipaul remarks, his distaste for politics manifest, " . . . a word of literary criticism like 'well-crafted' and 'honed'. When someone talks about something being 'crafted' or 'honed', and 'full of compassion', you know you must stay away."

Naipaul prefers to speak of the pursuit of happiness. "Familiar words, easy to take for granted; easy to misconstrue," he recently wrote. "I find it marvelous to contemplate to what an extent, after two centuries, and

after the terrible history of the earlier part of this century, the idea has
come to a kind of fruition . . . So much is contained in it: the idea of the
individual, responsibility, choice, the life of the intellect, the idea of
vocation and perfectibility and achievement. It is an immense human
idea. It cannot be reduced to a fixed system. It cannot generate fanati-
cism. But it is known to exist; and because of that, other more rigid
systems in the end blow away.''

The Ultimate Exile

Stephen Schiff / 1994

From *The New Yorker*, 23 May 1994, 60–71. Reprinted by permission of Stephen Schiff.

When Saul Bellow returned from a trip in London in the winter of 1982, he told friends about meeting the writer V. S. Naipaul for the first time. "After one look from him, I could skip Yom Kippur," Bellow said. Naipaul was fifty then, and he had spent decades developing his famously forbidding, admonitory presence—his "eagle-on-the-crags look," as Bellow puts it.

Photographs of him from the late fifties and early sixties, when he first emerged as a writer of deft comic novels and stories about his native Trinidad, show something different: a slender, boyish sprite, his walnut-colored skin almost dewy, his thick black hair flopping rakishly across his forehead, his eyes dreamy and gleaming. But in pictures taken only a few years later you see the man Bellow saw. The hooded eyes have become sulfurous and accusing, and they peer out warily from behind middens of flesh; the band of skin between them is clenched, and the mouth, so sensuous in earlier photographs, now tugs downward at the corners in a caricature of disdain. Naipaul the arrogant, Naipaul the severe.

Yet this was the Naipaul who, by the time Bellow met him, had gathered more praise than most writers accrue in a lifetime. Every few years, it seemed, he was short-listed for the Nobel Prize; critics commonly called him "Britain's greatest living writer," "the best novelist now writing," "our finest writer of the English sentence" (this from his frequent detractor the Nobel laureate Derek Walcott). His early fiction, written in a clipped, knowing style that seemed improbably disciplined and mature for a writer still in his twenties, had been terribly funny—and terribly poignant, too—about the yearnings of an island populace dimly convinced that real life was going on somewhere else. Those early books won awards, attracted tributes from the likes of Kingsley Amis and Anthony Powell, and were followed, in 1961, by a brilliant comic epic, *A House for Mr. Biswas*. Here was something genuinely new in the world: the Great West Indian Novel, a vigorous, prodigiously detailed account

135

of the frustrating life and early death of Naipaul's father, who had been a
struggling journalist in Trinidad. *A House for Mr. Biswas* was Dickensian
in its scope and sympathy, yet wholly original; it was both a robust
portrait of a peculiar community—the descendants of Uttar Pradesh
Brahmins who came west to Trinidad as indentured laborers—and a vivid
metaphor for the colonial predicament itself. Naipaul brought to it an eye
alert to both buffoonery and pain, and a lapidary, almost styleless
style—a style that marched from one plain description to the next,
avoiding music and show, steadily building a world. Although *A House
for Mr. Biswas* was never a bestseller, Naipaul's mastery was unmistak-
able. And he knew it. "My whole being was consumed with this thing,"
he told me recently. "I remember walking the streets to buy bread and
doing my shopping exalted. I knew I was carrying something wonderful."
Born in poverty, an East Indian of the West Indies—an exile twice
over—he had washed up in England, had gone through Oxford, had found
a prominent spot on the British literary map. And he was only twenty-
nine.

But something changed. After *A House for Mr. Biswas*, his writing
grew progressively gloomier. Novels like *The Mimic Men*, *In a Free
State* (which won England's Booker Prize), *Guerrillas*, and *A Bend in the
River* were corrosive, richly observed studies of the violence and degradation that have resulted, in Naipaul's view, from the sudden mingling of
First and Third World populations in the postwar era. The clownish
strivers of the early books gave way to a menagerie of lost souls, shattered
expatriates trying to build new lives in equally shattered lands, and
succumbing in the end to chaos, self-destruction, rape, and murder.
These were bleak, ominous books, marred by misanthropy and sexual
disgust, but Conradian in the way they explored the connections between
personal and political anarchy. And they were beautifully written: Naipaul created a pitiless poetry of ruined landscapes—of corrugated-iron
shanties, fetid rivers, cutlass-toting schoolboys, and distant, portentous
gunfire. The novels looked pessimistic then; now they look prophetic.
Meanwhile, books of history and travel, like *The Middle Passage* (about
the West Indies and South America), *An Area of Darkness* (about India),
The Loss of El Dorado (about Trinidad), and *Among the Believers* (about
Islam), gave Naipaul a new reputation: he was a scourge of the post-
colonial world; an uncompromising critic of every liberation movement,
every ideologue and revolutionary; and, to his enemies, a self-created
mandarin who sneered from on high at the "half-made" societies bobbing
in the wake of departing colonial powers. Many on the left hated him,
thought him racist and anti-Third Word. They objected to the way he

called certain groups "barbarian," certain societies "primitive" or "simple." And Naipaul didn't mind baiting his enemies, sometimes outrage-
ously. He was anything but politically correct.

Not long ago, sitting in the dining room of his cottage, in Wiltshire, I
asked him about the arguments that some of his foes had put forward.
His answer was extravagant and gorgeous and strange—a kind of dithyramb. "I never argue," he began. "I loathe argument. I observe, and I
think for a long time. My words are always well chosen. I'm not a
debater. How can I be concerned about people who don't like my work?
No, I can't cope with that. I can't cope with that. I don't *read* these
things. I don't even read when people tell me nice reviews. I'm nervous
of being made self-conscious. I've got to remain pure. You've got to move
on to remain pure. You've got to move on to the next piece of work in a
pure spirit. And I know that I am considerably more intelligent than the
squabbles raised around me. People are not intelligent enough in their
analysis of what's wrong with their societies. They only know about their
enemies. My attitude has always been different: that one must look
inward and understand why one is weak, why a culture like mine or like
the one in India, from which I come ancestrally—why they are so without
protection in the world. And this has taken me to a higher global
understanding of things."

Perhaps, I suggested, his new book was an attempt to address some of
his critics' accusations. *A Way in the World*, which Knopf is calling his
first novel in seven years (though it is being published in England not as a
novel but as a sequence), is a series of nine related stories, some clearly
autobiographical, some embodying new approaches to material he has
explored elsewhere, but all of them about people who are living a lie.
Most of his characters are visitors to the West Indies: travel writers;
would-be liberators; huge figures, like Sir Walter Raleigh and the nineteenth-century revolutionary Francisco de Miranda; and smaller ones,
like a Trinidadian Indian trying to pass himself off as a well-to-do
Venezuelan on an airplane. Much of the book is written in the form of
long monologues, and in these Naipaul evinces a sympathy for his fibbers
and dreamers and frauds which is unlike anything in his previous fiction.
Could his evident regard for the black Trinidadian character named Blair
or for the black Trinidadian revolutionary named Lebrun (transparently
based on the writer C. L. R. James) or for the Amerindian who tells
much of Raleigh's story—could these things have been a response to the
critics who had so over-simplified his work?

The dithyramb continued. "No. I don't want to talk about this. The
notes for this book—some of them were made seventeen years ago, and

it's been cogitated for a very long time. No. Writing isn't that. Writing isn't just being anti-African or anti-Negro—whatever. How on earth? It's absurd. The books have to look after themselves, and they will be around as long as people find that they are illuminating. Instead of coming to me and asking 'Why did you write this book?' you should be saying 'How did you see so much?' That should be the question. And the question might be 'Why do you have this eye—that you can point out the flaws in movements?' And I would say 'It is very easy to see the flaws in movements if you abolish sentimentality and you question everything that bothers you.' Simple people write simple things. The thing is, I am not a simple man. I have an interesting mind, a very analytical mind. And what I say tends to be interesting. And also very true. That's all that I can do about it. I can't lie. I can't serve a cause. I've never served a cause. A cause always corrupts.''

All this was said with some heat, and yet there was a surprising, practiced charm in it as well. I felt he wasn't raging at me; the implicit message was "We are not going to enjoy ourselves if you keep asking me questions like that, and if you don't we will.'' Naipaul's voice is a melodious baritone, as plangent as any actor's, and, like an actor, he uses it self-consciously, caressing words like "lie'' and "flaws,'' dropping into a whisper or a hiss, and then climbing to heights of ringing declamation. The accent is properly Oxonian, but with a lilt of the islands in it, and there is Naipaul's lovely, now famous affectation: the repetition of certain phrases, over and over, until they become soothing and chantlike and intimate. (Some have called it "the Naipaul bis,'' from the musical term for a passage that repeats.) What you say to him gets repeated, too, as if he were ingesting it, making it his own for later use, and he punctuates his conversation with disarming, conspiratorial asides—"You *know* these things. Yes. You *know* these things''—that sometimes implicate you in knowing things you don't know at all. At one point in our conversations, he said, "I did have for many years, when I was young, the feeling that if I didn't do my work I would find it very hard to eat. I hated the idea of eating at the end of the day.'' And then, looking at me sharply: "You don't know about this? You don't see it in your own life?'' I had to admit I did not.

I had approached him with some trepidation, because his scary fastidiousness has become legend. It was said that he was grossly intolerant of even a few minutes' tardiness, that if you asked him to dinner he would first demand a rundown of the menu (vegetarian only, please) and admonish you to serve good wine; it was said that he had reduced more than one ill-prepared journalist to tears, and that he was fond of remarking, "Never give anyone a second chance. When people have let you down, you can be sure they will do it again." He has a hair-trigger temper, and has been known to fly into long, excoriating rages, in restaurants, on airplanes, at hotels. Once, he abruptly changed publishing houses when he discovered himself listed in the spring catalogue as a "West Indian writer." On another occasion, a publisher flew him to Holland for a week-long series of press conferences and interviews, but the first questioner at the first conference posed a query he found unworthy, and—despite the lights, the cameras, and the assembled Dutch press—Naipaul walked out, had himself driven to the airport, and took the next plane back to England.

All these stories, and then that face—the face that so alarmed Bellow, with its tormented eyes and the grimace of displeasure at a world that could never measure up.

But the face I encountered was altogether different. Naipaul is nearly sixty-two now, and his eyes have grown smoky and mirthful, with wispy little sprigs above them instead of the beetling brows I had expected. He is small, narrow-boned, and elegant-looking, and his down-turned mouth looks not sour but witty, surrounded, as it is, by a salty beard that gives him an avuncular air. Even in the midst of his dithyramb, there is something gentle and coaxing in the way he speaks, almost like a plea for understanding; you can feel the anxiety welling behind his words—the very anxiety that must have given him his fearsome reputation through the years, boiling over into hysteria and bad behavior and fury. These days, he is more likely to retreat into laughter. "People think that one is a very serious, dour, gloomy man, but one is full of humor," he says. "That tome is always available to the writer. The humor is always available, waiting to bubble up, when it's needed."

That is how he talks, as if he were observing from afar the creature who bears his name. He says "one" instead of "I" he refers to himself as "the writer" and sometimes as "the man." "I do it instinctively, distinguishing between them, between writer and man," he says. Having been knighted in 1990, the man is now formally known as Sir Vidiadhar Surajprasad Naipaul, but he doesn't use the title. His friends call him Vidia, and so does his wife, Pat, whom he calls Patsy. She is a small, slender, handsome Englishwoman of about Naipaul's age, with gray hair that is cut in a pageboy and, behind big, round glasses, very wide-awake eyes. They met at Oxford and married in 1955, when Naipaul was twenty-two, and though she was briefly a schoolteacher during the years when Naipaul's books couldn't support them, she has since functioned as his organizer, his sometime researcher, his closest adviser. In even the most autobiographical of his books, Pat is never mentioned (a "companion" is referred to once in *An Area of Darkness*), but friends say she can be scrappy, rebuking her husband during his more unsavory rhetorical flights—he has been known, for instance, to demand corporal punishment for a tardy plumber, or to refer to people as "monkeys," "infies" (short for "inferiors"), and, occasionally, "bow-and-arrow men." (Critics crying "Racism!" should note that he deploys such terms against white, upper-middle-class Englishmen as readily as against blacks and Indians and Arabs.) Still, ever since my arrival at the Wiltshire house Pat has spent most of her time meekly serving—a fish lunch, a rhubarb pie, endless pots of tea. Often, she seems to be lurking in doorways, waiting to be granted an audience with the great man; it is the sort of relationship that has established its own grooves and rhythms, but an outsider is likely to find it disquieting.

Vidia, on the other hand, can be mischievous about it. One afternoon, he stops our conversation in midsentence to cock an ear toward what Pat is saying on the telephone in another room. "Women's voices!" he hisses. "I can't *stand* the sound of women's voices now. I turn the radio off when I hear a woman. I get very *irritated*. So you see. This is how far one has sunk." He giggles. It is the sort of outrageous statement that might be putty in the hands of his enemies, but I can't help noticing that he never demands agreement. Naipaul is aware of his eccentricities, even revels in them. He has always viewed himself as the ultimate exile, hence the ultimate oddity; by now, peculiarity has become a way of life. He has opinions on everything (including music, which he admits to me he knows absolutely nothing about), and he doesn't discriminate among his sentiments, doesn't select or censor. If he feels something, it must be expressed. And this is as true of the work as of the man: in his writing, too, no morsel of information, no thoughtful tangent is deemed extraneous. (The reader will sometimes disagree.)

He grew up in Port of Spain, in an enormous, anarchic family very like the one in *A House for Mr. Biswas*, and ever since, it seems, he has been searching for quiet and order and sense. He has never wanted children. "It really comes from a detestation of the squalling background of children that I grew up with in my extended family," he says. His books linger obsessively over the details of badly built dwellings, shoddy furniture, sloppy art; these reminders of the old chaos afflict him. He is finicky about noise, about food, about wine, about the temperature; his nerves seem raw, close to the surface. And, though he has always had very real troubles with asthma, he is a fanatical exerciser, a longtime devotee of a yogic maneuver known as the bridge, in which he stands and stretches himself back until his hands hit the floor, contorting his body into the shape of a Romanesque arch. After every book, he complains of profound fatigue. "I have no more than one hundred months left," he told me one evening. "One hundred months, I mean, of productive life. Yes. Yes. It's an immense relief to feel that you're near the end of things." He stared gravely into the middle distance. I didn't have the heart to tell him that I recalled his announcing the very same thing—a hundred more months of productive life—to a British interviewer in 1979, when he was forty-seven years old.

"Vidia is a sufferer," Diana Athill, who edited nineteen of his twenty-two books, says. "He was born with a skin or two too few. The thing about editing him was that you didn't actually ever have to do a single thing to any of his books. But you did have to do a lot of attempting to cheer him up, because he would deliver a book and he would be happy when he delivered it, and then really soon he would go into a pit: What is the point? What is the point of writing books? I'm never going to write another book, and no one knows how to publish books, and no one knows how to review books. And you would have to have long lunches in which you were trying to persuade him that life wasn't as hopeless as it appeared. We actually talked about this once when he was very low, and I said, 'Well, don't you get a feeling sometimes—I walk down the street and see the trees coming into leaf, and I get a feeling that makes life worth living.' And he said, 'Do you really? You're awfully lucky. It doesn't happen to me.' "

"He is depressive at time," his friend the writer Paul Theroux says. "But his other side is not manic—it's joyous. He actually said to me once, 'I have a great capacity for happiness.' But he also, literally, stays home, indoors, for weeks or months on end, just thinking, doing nothing more than developing a whole train of thought. I don't know anyone else quite like that." Not surprisingly, his acquaintances say they don't see much of him—and many of them have quarrelled with him. "He has a shrinking circle of friends," says Theroux, who, along with the critic Francis Wyndham and the London social figure Teresa Wells, remains among the loyal few. Although Naipaul has enjoyed more social life than he likes to let on—especially during the sixties and seventies, when, as he says, "I briefly frequented the circle around Antonia Fraser"—he has long kept aloof from the London literary establishment. In fact, he has spent most of his life working very hard: writing, travelling, and then writing still more about what his travels inspire. He is still close to his sisters (one of whom died in 1984, leaving four) and their children, and though he says he was not particularly intimate with his brother, Shiva, who was thirteen years his junior, friends recall a patriarchal—and rather rough—relationship. Like Vidia, Shiva went to Oxford, and, like Vidia, he became a writer; his first two novels, *Fireflies* and *The Chip-Chip Gatherers*, were well received. The trouble was that Shiva's view of the world was rather like his brother's and so were his travels (Africa, South America); he never fully emerged from Vidia's shadow.

"Before Shiva was at Oxford, Vidia was very helpful to him," Athill says. "But I once went to lunch, and it was Vidia, Pat, me, and Shiva. And in Vidia's eyes Shiva couldn't do anything right. He had this picture in his mind that Shiva was going to utterly disgrace himself and the family and that he was going to become a drug addict, was going to be useless. It was intense anxiety. He was cruel to the boy, really cruel telling him he was a fool whenever he said anything or did anything, really, to a point where Shiva was sitting there not daring to speak because if he said anything he was snipped at. I think Vidia loved him but he thought Shiva was going to come to some terrible end."

In a way, he was right. Overweight and a heavy smoker, Shiva died of a heart attack in 1985, at the age of forty. For Vidia, it was a colossal blow. "My body began to burn," he told me. "I was doing a television program, and my hands began to erupt. My body was covered with an eczema—the eczema of grief." When I saw him a few weeks ago he still retained a trace of it, a spot near the eye, and there were streaks of shiny, dark, chapped-looking skin, like oilslicks, high on his cheeks. These, he explained, had recently "adhered" to the original eczema. Standing in his living room, he solemnly wagged two fingers at the black streaks, as though delivering a curse. "Death," he said.

But Pat had overheard him. "Oh stop that," she ordered.

"Death has come to me and said 'You are mine,' " Vidia intoned, and while Pat sputtered protests, he burst into laughter.

He keeps two apartments in London—one an airy duplex with lots of polished blond wood, the other a tiny place he had had for over twenty years where, he says, "I go and sit and sometimes I take in the silence. Just to be alone. Not to hear voices." Most of the time, though, he is in Wiltshire, near Stonehenge and Salisbury, where he has lived for twenty-four years—first in a three-room cottage on the estate of the aesthete and recluse Stephen Tennant, and then, for the last twelve years, in a cottage of his own, a sturdy, two-story brick house with what seem like dozens of small rooms—most of them outfitted with desks and bookshelves, and strewn with papers. "I work in all the rooms," he says. "It's a house of work."

He writes slowly and painfully—as I can see when he shows me some of his notebooks. Flipping the pages, he says, "Look, these four words are all of April 19th. I spent a whole day doing that." He flips another page. "Ah, you see, the same paragraph being written, several versions of it. That's very good. I know by now that if I have a very good day it tends to be followed by a very bad day. Because I'm exhausted by my mind. Look at that. Look at that. In January, I really am suffering, you see: 'Bad night. Lost. Very low. But did exercise. 175.' That's a punishing number. A hundred and seventy-five bridges. That is killing oneself. That's murder. But it kept me alive. Yes. Yes. The exercises revive you."

Naipaul writes in longhand and then resorts to the computer. "It's seldom more than four hundred words a day," he says. "It's not in my brain to do more. You start in the morning, when you're free, and then lunch, and then you work in the evening before dinner. Dinner might be late if you're having a good burst. And the good burst would be just that little part of a page. That would be quite enough." I ask him whether he reads other people's books while working on his own. "I read some pages, but I don't finish books," he says. "I follow what Proust said: I get in touch with the music of the writer, and that's enough."

Proudly, he shows me his garden; there is a lot of lawn, some struggling trees, and a flourishing, diverse hedge. He fingers a familiar-looking shrub, tenderly. "It's holly, yes," he says. "I love the holly. I planted it for the red berries and the thorn. A little bit of one's childhood is coming out here—it's a Christmas thing. And do you know that in the Himalayas it is fed to camels?"

We tramp around for a while, with Naipaul explaining which plants are worthy and which are not. In this, as in everything else, he is a snob. "This almond I don't like—Betjeman has written about it. It looks like something from the garden center. Now, these are plum trees. These are things which I wouldn't do now, but visitors adore them—especially people from France. They're a kind of cherry blossom. To me, they're the quintessential suburban plant. But I was untutored, you see. The garden man said, 'What you need is a couple of cherry blossoms.' I loved the words—'cherry blossom,' you know?" He succumbs to a deep, chesty laugh. "But a sense comes to you. It's a sense. It's a *sense*, a *sense* of what is correct. What I don't have, and the English usually like, are flowers. They love flowers. I can't *bear* them. I can't bear them except in shops. The colors are too, too—I like grass and I like trees." He fingers an enormous shrub. "This has an orange berry. I don't like it. I don't like it."

Abruptly, he turns to me, a mysterious look on his face. "I don't work in the garden now," he says dramatically, and then waits a beat; so that I can ask him why. I know that he has recently had back surgery to remove some bone spurs. (It makes me wonder about all those bridges.) But could that be the reason? "I've fallen out of love with it," he says, sighing profoundly. "I've fallen out of love with Wiltshire. It was a wonderful thing, living here. It helped me to do my work, gave me the solitude and the quiet which I cherish, and the space. All that has gone wrong is that one has fallen out of love. And when I fall out of love with places I just hide from them. I'm thinking that probably it might be time to move on."

By now, he is more Wiltshire than Trinidad—he has even lived here longer—but Trinidad remains his obsession, his crown of thorns. He may, in fact, have written about it a few times too often. "It's quite helpless, really," he says. "I can't do otherwise. I've lived there so long mentally. That leaving home was an immensity. I've been trying all my life to express that, the bigness of that. The central experience of my life." He was born in the country town of Chaguanas, on August 17, 1932; his grandfather, a Brahmin from the Gangetic Plain, had come there as an agricultural laborer. Vidia's father, Seepersad, whom he adored, was a high-strung man, prone to mental illness and breakdown; he was a journalist at the *Trinidad Guardian* and an impassioned, frustrated writer of short stories. Vidia has always credited him with inspiring his own drive to be a writer, but in many ways it was Vidia's mother who was the dominating force: she came from a rich, enormous family, the Capildeos, with whom Vidia and his parents were often forced to live. "I suffered so much from those relationships," he says. "The family quarrels—I suffered immense torment about it, and that was linked with my wish to have my own space, to be away."

As a teen-ager, he became aloof, proud, satirical, rather like the boy Anand in *A House for Mr. Biswas*, and some of the bulwarks that he devised against the discord around him stood him in good stead. In particular, he developed a memory exercise that he called "playing the newsreel back," which he has described as "trying to remember words, gestures and expressions in correct sequence, to arrive at an understanding of people I had been with and the true meaning of what had been said." Groping for order, he taught himself to interpret handwriting, and even to read faces in an unusual way. "You learn to associate a kind of face with a kind of human behavior," he says. "So you store a lot. I don't keep a journal, because I prefer to let memory do its sifting. Otherwise, the detail and the self-consciousness of the journal will get in the way. And I remember something else. I would talk very fast as a child. I was famous for it. I would talk so fast that I would have the time to mouth again what I had said. I was about eight or nine at the time. Did it for a long time. I would speak a sentence, and I would repeat it to myself—the second time was silent. I think I was probably just checking, checking.'' The birth of the bis, perhaps.

Naipaul grew to hate what he viewed as the stunted life of colonial Trinidad, and the moment he could get out he did. In 1950, a scholarship sent him to University College, Oxford. "He was very nervous at first," Peter Bayley, his tutor, remembers. "But everyone recognized him as a remarkable person." His first-term report read: "Fluent and quick in thought and writing: sometimes too cavalier and blasé. This slightly contemptuous attitude could be a potential danger." Naipaul says he was popular at college, but he also remembers it as a time of misery, and in 1952 he suffered a mental breakdown. "It was solitude and wretchedness and depression—every thing, every kind of obvious thing," he says. "They were wretched years—don't want to relive them at all. From when I left home, in '50, which I so much wanted to do, to about '58 or so was really a pretty dreadful period. Before I became secure as a writer, it was a long, unbroken period of melancholy."

He has written about the sorrow he experienced at his father's death—in 1953, when Vidia was twenty-one—and about the displacement he felt when he returned to Trinidad in 1956, only to scurry back to London, where, he now knew, he would try to make his career. He had married Pat by then, and was struggling to write, but he felt lost and unauthentic, and he was very, very poor. But there was something else as well. "There was a kind of tremendous sexual *soif*, very unfulfilled," he says. "And I was a very passionate man. I wasn't spurned; it was incompetence. I didn't know how to seduce the girl. There were many girls who were very friendly, and I didn't know how to cope with it. I was untutored. One would like to drive forward, but I didn't know how. I didn't know about the physical act of seduction, you see. I didn't know, because I'd never been told. I was too shy. And I don't know how people learn about the act of seduction, really; I still don't know. So I became a great prostitute man, which, as you know, is highly unsatisfactory. It's the most unsatisfying form of sex. Terrible. There is nothing in it." He is vehement now, almost hissing the words. "It's nothing; it's worthless. However much you tell yourself otherwise, it's worthless."

I mention his having been married throughout this period. "The one doesn't include the other," replies. "But learning about seduction and satisfying is almost like learning how to write. I was an extremely passionate man, and utterly heterosexual—an adorer of women, all my life. What has happened now is that, with age, women have sunk in my

esteem quite a bit. I'm no longer blinded by this way of looking at them.
So in a way that's a kind of loss. One has lost this excitement about
women. And probably one could say this about Muslim countries and
other countries—that since old men make the laws, the laws tend to be
rather harsh about women, because the blinding has faded away. But I
adored women. I thought they were wonderful. I loved their voices. I
loved the quality of their skin. I loved everything about them."

The books don't show it. Women have little place in them, and, when
they appear, lust often degenerates into revulsion. Naipaul's friends
remember periods when he swore off sex completely. "His sexual disgust
is easily aroused," Paul Theroux says. "Sex disgusts him, and the things
people eat, the way they look, how they smell. The disgust is very, very
strong. A lot of the reminders of ordinary humanity—people tapping their
feet to music, being aroused when a woman walks by, these things that
are examples of people losing control—disgust him. They remind him of
all the things he hated about Trinidad. They remind him of carnival time
on the island."

Eventually, though, during a trip to Argentina in the seventies, Naipaul's fortunes altered. "The sexual ease came quite late to me," he
says. "And it came as an immense passion. Conrad has a lovely line: 'A
man to whom love comes late, not as the most splendid of illusions, but
like an enlightening and priceless misfortune.' So that came to me. And I
feel that a lot of my creative energy has come from that. I'm most
grateful, yes, I'm delighted to have had it. It would have been terrible to
have died without it. So that didn't destroy the writer—it built him up a
little bit. She was someone who didn't care a damn about my work,
who'd never heard of me. Still hasn't read all of them—not all, not all."
Her name was Margaret, and she was an Argentine of British descent, a
slender, attractive married woman (with three children) who was about
ten years younger than Naipaul, and several inches taller. "Their meeting
was instant magnetism," a friend says. "Their eyes just sort of locked."
Remarkably, although Margaret doesn't live in England, the relationship
has continued over the years; she often joined Naipaul during his travels,
and she stayed with him during the two semesters in the late seventies
when he taught at Wesleyan University in Connecticut.

By that time, of course, he was a famous man, but financial well-being
was a long time in coming. His books didn't attract notice in America
until he published *Guerrillas* here in the mid-seventies—nearly twenty
years after his first novel *The Mystic Masseur*, appeared in England. And
though he is financially comfortable now, he knows he will never be a
best-seller; in fact, money is something of an obsession with him. He

likes to quiz people about it; he once perturbed the film maker George
Lucas asking him just how much he made. Pointing to his house in
Wiltshire Naipaul told me, "I paid all of forty-four thousand pounds for
it—that's eight, eight thousand dollars. In 1979." He laughed hugely.
"This gave me the reputation of being a very shrewd man, a very
shrewd investor."

That was fifteen years ago. I moved into the house three years later,
and the twelve years he has been there have produced a profound change
in his work. If the comic novels and stories about Trinidad, climaxing
with *A House for Mr. Biswas*, constituted the early period, and the
blistering fiction and nonfictions about exile and alienation in the Third
World constituted middle period, then the last ten years have introduced
an adventurous new phase. With *Finding the Center*, in 1984, Naipaul
began to write more directly about his own life: about his boyhood; about
his early attempts to will himself into his vocation; about the torturous
path he took toward discovering his form and his voice. Naipaul had
always been regarded as a rather traditional storyteller, but in the early
eighties he began to tinker with the form, and in 1987 he produced a
strange and beautiful "novel"—a masterpiece, in fact, called *The Enigma
of Arrival*. Dense difficult, yet oddly tender, the book rewarded study
more than casual reading. At first glance, it seemed to be half autobiography—once again, the trials of the clueless colonial learning to write and
half a portrait of Wiltshire life: Naipaul's cottage, the grounds, neighbors,
their woes. The incidents he was describing were banal, seemingly
unworthy of Naipaul's redoubtable eye. But the writing had a slow,
almost Mahleresque majesty—something that Naipaul had never quite
achieved before. It came at the reader in repeating waves, depositing bits
of information, and then receding, only to surge forward again, a little
farther this time, depositing a little bit more. Gradually, you came to
realize that Naipaul was writing about nothing less than the life of the
mind—but in an almost epistemological sense. He was letting his reader
in on the writer's way of knowing, of piecing together what he sees,
drawing conclusions, tearing them up, emending them, seeing more. Far
from being a traditional novel *The Enigma of Arrival* was a cutaway view
of narrative itself, as though the story it told were just a crust beneath
which the reader could watch the shifting plates of a writer's consciousness.

His journalism had prepared him. He had spent years trekking through
Africa, India, South America, the Near and Far East, observing and
interviewing, writing exact descriptions and analyses of what he saw, and
then turning around a few years later and reworking them into fictions.

An article entitled *The Killings in Trinidad*, about the depredations of a would-be revolutionary who called himself Michael X, was transmuted into *Guerrillas*, and an article about Mobutu and the Congo grew into *A Bend in the River*. Naipaul was never an inventor of material, always a transformer; he had little respect for many of the time-honored building blocks of fiction—myth, fantasy, fairy tale, invention, even the gift of storytelling itself. "I wouldn't know what the point of all that is," he told me. "I don't want to be excited by suspense—I don't need that kind of thing." And myth? Fairy tale? "Un*bear*able. Have you tried reading the Grimms' fairy tales in any bulk? Un*bear*able. Too irrational. You can go on forever. It's like a Henry Moore sculpture—you can just add things all the time. There's no reason it should ever stop. It's too arbitrary. And it doesn't illuminate anything. I think the early people who used the fictional form used it to illuminate things that the other forms couldn't do. To write about the Russian society, you would only have had the official report or the travel book. So you need another kind of writing to explore it. And without Balzac people wouldn't have understood what France had become. But that's done. You can't go and do it again."

Narrative, though, is something different. "It occurs all the time," Naipaul said. "Your coming here is narrative. You know, the man who drove you here is narrative. It's all narrative. It's a matter of choosing. It's when you're doing the other kind of writing—you start looking for a thing called plot and you get into trouble, you know? Narrative is something large going on around you all the time. Plot is something so trivial—people want it for television plays. Plot assumes that the world has been explored and now this thing, plot, has to be added on. Whereas I am still exploring the world. And there is narrative there, in every exploration. The writers of plots know the world. I don't know the world yet. I began to understand that quite late. I began to understand the full richness of the world that I was in the middle of, and how to go about it."

What he understood might have eluded another writer, but Naipaul had prepared his own way well. Moving from Oxford to London in 1954, taking jobs at the BBC and at the Cement-and-Concrete Association (writing public-relations copy) to support himself, he aspired to become a writer, without really having anything to write about. His first approach was to pretend to be something he was not—a cosmopolitan Londoner, not an Indian from Trinidad who had grown up in what he persists in calling "the bush." Slowly, he found his way; slowly, he learned to let his memory, rather than his pretension, speak. But what disturbed him most was the stricture of form—the need to produce plots, stories, characters, the traditional rhythms of the novel. "What was worrying me

was the unnaturalness of it,'' he says. "It was: Why am I doing this?
Why do I have to write these invented stories? And it worried me how to
move on. And I remember I was on a trip to India, nervous about going
on as a writer. And on the freighter I began to be worried, almost in the
way of neurosis, that I was losing the gift of speech. Very few passengers,
and I had that fear. This is the depth of one's worry. But now all my
forms are my own. I will not let anyone tell me that I must have people
coming in through the door and describe the room, and then, you know,
the kind of writing where you have one operative line in a paragraph, or
you have one in a page, so people know what's happening. Page 1: He's
coming to the flat. Page 2: There is a banker in the flat. And it goes on
like that. No, my writing is something else now. It is carefully done, like
a watch.''

He is a great hater of style in prose. "I don't like things where the
writer is not to be there. The writer has to take me, rather like Pepys.
He's not there; I have to read through him. Santayana: almost unreada-
ble. Gibbon lulls one to sleep. The King James Bible: unbearable—
un*bear*able. The rhythm, and the killing of sense, the killing of sense. I
like good, brambly writers. Richard Jefferies—he's a good writer. So
many observations, knitted in very quickly. Sharp, edgy; the writing
seems a little awkward, but in fact a lot is being delivered. I don't like
smooth things—I can't bear smoothness. Dryden is smooth. And I dislike
things with rhythm. I think prose shouldn't have rhythm. The writer
should break it up if he spots it—break it up! In my writing, there's no
self-consciousness, there's no beauty. The writer is saying, 'Pay attention. Everything is here for a purpose. Please don't hurry through it.' If
you race through it, of course you can't get it, because it was written so
slowly. It requires another kind of reading. You must read it at the rate,
perhaps, at which the writer himself likes to read books. Twenty, thirty
pages a day, because you can't cope with more. You've got to rest after
reading twenty good pages. You've got to stop and think. I read very
slowly. It's very natural. My paragraphs are very rich—they have to be
read. Many things are happening in the paragraph. If you miss a paragraph—if you miss a page—it's hard to get back into it.''

This is especially true of *The Enigma of Arrival* and the books that
have followed it. With *A Turn in the South* (1989), a record of his journey
through the Southern United States, and *India: A Million Mutinies Now*
(1990), the third in a trilogy of travel books about that country, Naipaul
began to rely more and more on interviews, on building a collage out of
dozens of voices, with his own voice providing dense, analytical commen-
tary in between. The books are surprisingly gentle, almost anodyne; they

reveal a writer whom age and experience have tempered. In *A Turn in the South* Naipaul is virtually gaga about the redneck culture and country-music lyrics and black church choirs. There is little about racism in it. And in *A Million Mutinies Now* the horror and contempt that racked *An Area of Darkness* and *India: A Wounded Civilization* have been replaced by a kind of hope: unlike practically any other recent observer of the subcontinent, Naipaul feels encouraged by a newly literate India's awakening to its own history, even if that awakening arouses rage.

These books lead up to the new one, *A Way in the World*, in which Naipaul attempts to transfer the nonfiction technique he has developed—the collage of voices—to a work of fiction. It's a bumpy ride. Although Naipaul has in the past proved himself adept at capturing the sound of Trinidad's pidgin, and even of American Southern accents, the voices in this book—whether of a Trinidadian schoolteacher, a seventeenth-century Amerindian, or Francisco de Miranda himself—all sound like Naipaul and not like Naipaul talking but like Naipaul writing. The sections he is happiest with are the longest ones, about Raleigh and Miranda, but they prove the least convincing: in forcing the historical characters to recount their own histories, Naipaul hoped to bring a new emotion and a new empathy to tales he had already told in *The Loss of El Dorado*, but instead he has found himself falling between two stools: the historical details feel sketchy; the emotion feels wan and trumped up.

Still, Naipaul is terribly proud of this book—"I will be quite content if this is my last work, quite content," he told me—and there is a lot here to be proud of. Almost everything in its nine disparate sections links up with everything else, and what emerges is a kind of chain in four dimensions, coiled and crisscrossed over the centuries, enmeshing dozens of lives and fates that happened to traverse a single West Indian patch of land and sea. For all its flaws, *A Way in the World* is a true summing up. In it Naipaul musters a compassion that is a very far cry from the sullenness of the middle period: here his sympathy can encompass slaves, revolutionaries, aboriginals, and white marauders alike, because all of them are victims—victims of the dreams, lies, lusts, and rages that are, in Naipaul's view, the true forces of history. In fact, it is history itself that is the protagonist here, and Naipaul keeps twisting it in the light like a crystal, letting its various facets glint. In one passage he describes returning to Port of Spain in the aftermath of a bloody rebellion in 1990, a rebellion that spread and subsided in the very streets and buildings where, years before, he had worked as a clerk, making copies of birth, marriage, and death certificates—the documents of history:

It was unsettling to see what had been city—regulated, serviced, protected, full of wonder and the possibility of adventure—turn to vacancy, simple ground. The commercial streets of the centre had been levelled. You could see down to what might have been thought buried forever: the thick-walled eighteenth-century Spanish foundations of some buildings. You could see the low gable marks of early, small buildings against higher walls. You could look down, in fact, at more than Spanish foundations: you could look down at red Amerindian soil.

The perpetuity of history: if Naipaul could be said to have a religion, that would be its ruling tenet. For him, the knowledge of history is a humanizing influence—humanizing in the sense of making humane. Writing about Islamic fundamentalism, in an essay called "Our Universal Civilization," he says, "The faith abolished the past. And when the past was abolished like this, more than an idea of history suffered. Human behavior, and ideals of good behavior, could suffer." History for Naipaul is a kind of order, a bastion against the chaos, personal and political, that he has despised all his life—ever since he found himself in the midst of it, among the squalling children and carnival lights back in Port of Spain.

And here is where his argument against those who wish to save the Third World begins. Most such saviours are ideologues, and Naipaul hates any ideology—Marxist, Maoist, Muslim, or Africanist—that wishes to wipe away history. He values order, yes, but order alone is not enough; he prefers India, where there are "a million mutinies now," to the Iran of the fundamentalists, where order itself has become a kind of chaos—by being arbitrary, by being illogical, by being deaf to human need. Naipaul's detractors have seen him as a sort of uppity wog, a dark-skinned colonial "passing" as a pillar of the empire—or, to use Edward Said's word, a "scavenger." This is a large oversimplification. It is true that Naipaul has regarded most indigenous Third World liberators with a cold eye, but history has borne him out on that point, and there is nothing in his work that suggests a love of imperialism. It is also true that Naipaul has been squeamish about, and even contemptuous of, Third World squalor. That, I think, is a matter of temperament more than a matter of belief. Naipaul was brought up a colonial in a caste society; he was reared with a thousand associations that made his skin crawl; he is a neurotic, a fussbudget—and that is the sort of characteristic that no amount of "progressive" thinking can be expected to alter. He cannot necessarily bring himself to enjoy the company of victims, but victims are not what enrages him; what enrages him is the societies that victimize. After all, he has been there.

In his London apartment one day, he showed me a few of the magnificent Indian paintings he collects. His aesthetic is consistent: in art, as in writing, he has very little use for invention, stylization, or charm. What he admires is skill, naturalism, observation, draftsmanship: order. A critic of a certain kind might call this bias of his Western, or European, but the art he showed me belied that notion: it may not be "charmingly" Indian, but Indian it is. And then he said something very interesting. We were looking at a delicate portrait of Shah Jahan, the builder of the Taj Mahal. "I think the most important thing about that picture is its condition," Naipaul said. "The eyes, the lips, the ears—very fine. But then it's so damaged around the head. And it's awful to say that within a hundred years of that picture being done and being locked away in the prince's library, it was plundered. And it was because that prince hadn't created a state. He hadn't created institutions to protect the painting, and, in a similar way, he hadn't protected his people. All that art, all that training, all that talent, and it's for the prince alone. It doesn't educate the country—it's part of nothing else, because the prince has provided nothing that will remain when he has been wiped away. When I make this point to scholars of Indian art, they think I'm making some antique point about Indians being barbarous and uncivilized. They're incapable of understanding what I'm saying—that all that energy should have gone into creating a self-aware, analytical society with its own intellectual possibilities."

Is Naipaul, then, a lover of Western civilization, of the civilization now frequently derided as having been built by dead white males? He is, unashamedly, but not because of any racial bias. As I read his work, it occurs to me that his litmus test for a desirable society would be as deceptively simple as this: Is it a society that someone like V. S. Naipaul could be a writer in? That is not a bad criterion. For instance, would he have the freedom to write, regardless of his origins? Could he become educated enough to write, also regardless of his origins? Would the society be intellectually alive enough to produce readers? Would its economy and system of government allow publication? Finally—and here even we are in danger—would the society make him want to write, and write well? Would it make producing good writing seem a desirable pursuit?

This last requisite, of course, was available to Naipaul even in Trinidad, thanks to his father's influence. It is the thing that brought him to England. But now I have one more question for him. He has talked of starting out poor, of being miserable and sexually incompetent. Yet I still can't fathom the pain that turned the boyish sprite in that early photograph into the baleful, stringent presence that so took Bellow aback. Young writers have always put themselves through hell. Was Naipaul's hell any worse?

He ponders for a moment. Then he says, "It was that I had no gift. I had no natural talent. I was waiting for something to come, waiting for it to infuse me, to enter me. And, of course, it isn't like that. So my writing was always learned. And I think the body of work exists because there was no natural gift. I think if I had had a natural gift it would have been for mimicry. I would have been mimicking other people's forms. No, I really had to work. I had to learn it. Having to learn it, I became my own man."

But if he had no natural talent, how could he have surpassed so many others—others putatively more gifted than he? Was it just hard work?

"Not that alone," he says. "There was also the element of panic. I was more frightened than anybody else. I *had* to do it. Other people have other causes of self-esteem, which they always bring into play. I had none. Other people think about their money, their background, their education, their motorcars. I didn't. You say you want to be a writer, you want to be a writer. How do you start? You sit down and you pretend you are writing. But it is so dreadful to pretend you are writing. What are you doing? Well, I think I'm writing. And then the day comes when you don't say, 'I think I'm writing.' You say, 'I'm working.' Big day. Very big day. Others didn't have the panic. But I had to become a writer very fast. I had to learn it. I had nothing else."

Delivering the Truth: An
Interview with V. S. Naipaul

Aamer Hussein / 1994

From *Times Literary Supplement*, 2 September 1994, 3–4. Reprinted by permission of Aamer Hussein.

Aamer Hussein: *You have recently spoken of narrative forms other than fiction being, in some cases and contexts, as creative as fiction, and much of your recent work is fact and document. Yet* A Way in the World, *your newest book, is again classified as a novel. Does your attitude signal, in some way, a change of direction in your imaginative writing?*

V. S. Naipaul: You have to write a different book from thirty years ago: you can't write the same book. Because you change, your knowledge of the world changes, and the forms have to change to meet the demands of the material you've accumulated. We can be burdened by dead forms. I was having a look, purely by accident, at Virginia Woolf's book of essays, *The Common Reader.* She was very exercised about the essay, which at the time she was writing had really been dead for seventy-five years, but, in 1919 or thereabouts, it still seemed as though it were a living form: people were practicing the essay. And it's just not true about the fictional form, people behaving as though it's the final form: it's a comparatively new form, as practiced. The dominant form at the beginning of the nineteenth century was the essay, surely. And then it altered. Because the novel became the way people could deliver truths they couldn't in any other way about society—mental states, and so on. It was all new; you might say that the novel dealt in news. In this way, the invented narrative made sense. The virtue didn't lie in the invention alone.

AH: *And when do you feel that you would rather invent, even if you've observed, seen, experienced something; how do you choose between a photographic replication of reality and fiction?*

VSN: To deliver the truth, really, to deliver a form of reality. Because if you were dealing with real people, when you start writing about them, it becomes too particular: and one wants to make a larger point, so you fabricate.

This book [*A Way in the World*] is a way of dealing with all the various strands of the Caribbean or New World background, the place, and all the different stages of learning about it, as well. The learning is important, and the form I've arrived at seems to me truer and more natural than any artificial narrative which would have tried to create a James Michener kind of connected story. My story does have connections; they are associations. They are inseparable from the background.

AH: *Images recur constantly, and characters are referred to in different periods . . .*

VSN: And with this form everyone will read his own book, depending on his nature, depending on his need. Some people might pick up certain half-buried associations and not see others that are more prominent. And I will tell you that this is also true of the writer. I would say this is one of the beauties of imaginative writing; you have two or three things you want to do consciously, but if, in the writing, you arrive at a certain degree of intensity, all kinds of other things occur which you're not aware of. I am still becoming aware of links between things, many months after writing. It may seem strange, but I didn't know the theme of revolution—and the idea of the revolutionary as a damaged man—was so dominant.

The writer must not review himself too much; but one of the themes at the back of my mind was the difficulty of being a writer with that background. In the beginning, it seemed to me very hard. But now, if I were an English person trying to be a writer, I wouldn't know how to start. I don't see how you can write about England without falling into parody, without competing with what you've read, without wishing to show that you know it too—class, sex, and so on.

There is no void here. The very opposite. The novel form has done its work. The true novelists today are people like Edwina Currie, Jeffrey Archer, John le Carré, Ken Follett. These are the giants of the novel today, presenting the public less with news than with novelties that they can romp through in the Underground train. People would say that there have always been popular writers, and that doesn't affect a thing called the literary novel, but I feel that the blockbuster—with its elements of the joke, and personal display, not unsophisticated—shows how the form has developed, and it has changed the attitude to fiction. The literary novel is delivering, nowadays, a kind of minor extravaganza itself, with, sometimes, major personal display. The idea of pinning down reality isn't really there. It's migrated perhaps to other forms. Perhaps something like the essay will give people reality about our confused, mixed world.

AH: *Do you find it rewarding to blur, or discount, the boundary between the fiction and the essay, to cast the fiction as an essay or vice versa?*

VSN: That's not new at all. Everyone knows who Proust is: when you read Proust, you don't think this is written by a person you know nothing about. It comes with Proust's myth, his legend. Maugham even provides his own legend in every story, Maugham the traveller, the cynical playwright, the sentimental teacher, the man who is not at all fazed by anything that human beings do. When I first began to write, I very soon felt the need to identify who the writer was, who was doing his travelling in the world, who was doing his observation of London or wherever. You couldn't suppress yourself. I made errors; I threw away good material. In the past few months, it's been tormenting me more and more. I wrote a book in 1962 called *Mr. Stone and the Knights Companion*, the first book I wrote set in London. I like the excellent material, still, but I feel it was thrown away by my suppression of the narrator, the observer who was an essential part of the story. To write a book as though you were this third-person omniscient narrator who didn't identify himself was in a way to be fraudulent to the material, which was obtained by me, a colonial, living precariously in London in a blank and anxious time, observing these elderly Edwardian people trying to postpone death. The house was stuffed with furniture from their previous marriages. The story is really the other story as well. This idea of point of view, of forms not intruding one on the other, made me throw away that material.

AH: *Because of conventional expectations?*

VSN: And an absurd idea of the form. I've been so obsessed by the wrongness of my approach to that material, the idea of the divine and unseen creator, that I might do something about it, rework it in some way.

It immediately comes to me when I open a conventional new book that this form of novel-writing is very theatrical, very operatic, with snatches of dialogue between paragraphs of description or dawdle. It derives, I think, from the nineteenth-century theatre. It has very little relation to reality. People don't talk like that or see like that. It's as stylized as eighteenth-century rhyming verse. It's what happens at the end of a form.

Many of the great novels were written in about sixty years of the nineteenth century, a long time for any culture. Those sixty years take in all the great work of Dostoevsky, Gogol, Turgenev, Balzac, Flaubert . . . things are racing away, and the great writers like Flaubert don't want to repeat what they've done. *Madame Bovary* is an unbearably beautiful work. Not only narrative and social truth and language, but the selection and achievement of detail. You can't do that again; it's like asking someone to write Proust again. So all these enormous developments take place, and the whole world learns how to write novels. But the people who come later are writing other people's novels, giving versions of the same.

AH: *Joyce, Woolf, Lawrence?*

VSN: Lawrence has one quality which is interesting: he introduced people to the idea of their sexuality. Woolf I don't know; Joyce is experimental, which deters me. He is also a blind person dealing with a different world from the one I inhabit because of his blindness.

AH: *Internal worlds, dream-worlds rather than debates or dialogues with the real?*

VSN: A double blindness perhaps. I cannot feel I've come to the end of the real world. I travel, see a lot more, I carry many more cultures in my head, and these people are much more restricted. They come from the imperial period—it's as simple as that—without knowing it, without considering themselves imperial writers. They inhabit a world where you don't see the other half or three-quarters. For that reason, they think reality's all been charted.

We should rethink all forms, not only fiction: academic work, history and travel books especially. You have only to look at Chekhov's book about the prison island of Sakhalin. He wanted to make the journey from point A back to point A, and to give all the facts and the figures and the tables. That was what the travel writers of the period were required to do. And the real work, then, what might have been the Chekhovian work, is abandoned to the footnotes. We lost a book because the writer didn't rethink the form.

AH: *That reminds me of the way some of your chapters and shorter pieces are entitled "unwritten" stories, but are actually very dense, written stories . . . .*

VSN: "Unwritten" because they are at once historical and invented. There's a crust of fact, but within that the writer's fantasy is working. It isn't being presented as anything else.

AH: What impulse takes you, now, away from imaginative works to those that can be classified as straightforward documentary or oral histories, in the case of your recent book on India?

VSN: That book on India [*India: A Million Mutinies Now*] is not oral history: it's an account of a civilization at a hinge moment. It's done through human experience; there's a special shape to the book, it's held together by a thread of inquiry, it's very carefully composed. The idea came to me that the truth about India wasn't what I thought about India, it's what they are living through. That is the great discovery; I moved to it slowly through earlier books, the books about the Islamic countries and the Deep South. I arrived at that form in the South, when people were describing to me what they felt; I was so excited by what I discovered. I'd never known about music and religion as supports against anarchy. I'd never understood it. That southern method was applied to

the Indian book. The travel book for me has also been a process of
learning. It's much more than oral history. A lot of the work lay in the
actual travel, and the day-to-day thinking.

To come back to the original question, I'm moved by two things: if I'm
writing a book like the Indian book, I'm passionate about accuracy. I'll
never alter a word that people spoke; I take it down by hand, and I don't
change it. Then there is another kind of imaginative truth which one
wants to get at. For example in my new book there is a special achievement—you may not be aware of it—from my point of view, in Miranda's
story, "In the Gulf of Desolation." All these statements are personal;
I'm not one to lay down the law. For twenty-five years also I've wanted
to portray the slave society, the new society that had been created with
its new calendars on this aboriginal land, and was the parent of the one I
grew up in. I did it here indirectly. Miranda, coming home after thirty-
five years, doesn't see Negroes. What happens is that in the middle of his
first day he hears people outside talking a strange language, and when he
goes to the window he sees Africans working in the grounds. Later, when
he returns, he again doesn't see. He just comes to the plantation house,
and he smells the cocoa beans sweating—it's a smell from his childhood—
and he sees the girls in the distance moving strangely, dragging their feet
through the drying beans. That was work, to arrive at that solution: to
have the slaves always there, but not true presences: an imaginative
moment for me, moving around in this new calendar. Also imaginatively
to show how you get corrupt, how your cause remains clear to you, but
you make all kinds of adaptations that other people judge you by. There
are two kinds of truths: I couldn't take the real life I saw in Wiltshire and
hang philosophical ideas about change on it. You can't do it, legally or
imaginatively, so you create your own construct, which sums up the
truth, to talk about flux and so on.

AH: *A basic, or speculative question: perhaps when you're recovering
a lost history, looking at its margins and blank spaces, an imaginative
reconstruction becomes more essential, and when you're trying to witness something that's happening now, you need a documentary
treatment?*

VSN: . . . and they're both truths.

AH: *You're sometimes diffident about your own interpretation of your
work, about laws laid down by you, and as someone who doesn't
subscribe to the idea of the death of the author, I wanted to ask you
about your own stance: your own passion for words, and what you put
into them, seems to remain of primary importance when you address
your work.*

VSN: But I also know that there are many writers and many kinds of writing, the world is very varied, and writing also has to be very varied. Shall we say this form where the material is linked together by associations—that begin very simply and then radiate through the text—is very good for this particular material. But it comes at the end of a lifetime's practice and cannot be recommended to someone else. Everyone has to find his own way. I like when I pick up a writer's book to find something entirely original, someone doing their own work.

AH: *Is there anyone working today, contemporaries in any genre, whose work you admire, or read for pleasure?*

VSN: You catch me out. At the moment, I'm reading a lot of Latin texts in the Loeb editions. That's a special interest, really a kind of idleness. I read the past a lot, to fill in the gaps. I like Ibsen, a very, very grand writer. The man moving on and on, and becoming quite mad at the end, but why not? I like Pepys, a great new discovery: one of the greatest English writers. And Balzac, of course. Flaubert's *Madame Bovary*: almost a life study, I think, one can read a page a month.

AH: *Poetry?*

VSN: I like MacNeice. There's a lot of feeling there that I can share. . . .

AH: *Are you conscious of a poet's impulse in your own work?*

VSN: I try to avoid it, to destroy it, in fact. I have no gift for poetry; if it's there, it's done accidentally, or contrary to my knowledge.

AH: *But not to your distaste, I hope, once it's there.*

VSN: I'm worried about too many beautiful thoughts. I've already mentioned Woolf. . . .

AH: *But you've recently virtually meditated about certain paintings.*

VSN: Indian art, especially, I've got to know more. I've begun to think that my feeling for realism may be part of my Indian inheritance. Because Indian painting can be awfully realistic. A common view is that it is formal and decorative, but just look, for example, at this very small painting of the Emperor Aurangzeb besieging a hill fort in the Deccan, just before 1700. All the horses, the men firing the muskets there from protected carts. The bullocks have been unyoked from the carts and are sitting with their backs to the battle. Here the camels are squatting, muskets have been mounted on their backs. This is an account of war. An extraordinary thing to have seized on so many details, long before the camera. There is a horse, lifting its right leg, the way horses do. You could use this picture to write an essay on Indian warfare.

AH: *There's also the painting by de Chirico that gives its title to* The Enigma of Arrival, *and creates narratives around it, of vision and* *revision; and, in the new book, there is an allusion to the Japanese printmaker Hokusai.*

VSN: Very beautiful. Hokusai woodcuts give the essence of a view in strokes and dots. He's quite different from the realism I'm talking about: he's very inventive and playful, and sometimes false and not so good. Sometimes a waterfall makes no sense.

AH: *So you create your own vision as you look at such work, like readers with your books.*

VSN: Reading new work is actually very hard. A good critic is someone who reads a text with a clear mind; most people are merely reading to find out what they already know.

Twenty-five years ago, when I was working on *In a Free State*, I determined to simplify the African landscapes I was using, and just choose a few elements and stress them repeatedly at different stages, to give the reader the illusion of knowledge. The reader creates his own landscapes anyway. So I thought I would give him something very formal to work with.

AH: *Sketched in strokes, rather than painted in heavy colours?*

VSN: And I like to repeat things in different ways. I like the reader to remember. Miranda's story is done four times. The idea is that an illusion of knowledge makes it easier for the reader to approach unfamiliar material. The writer's life is full of these moments, these decisions, like a painter's. There are many ironies in that Miranda story.

AH: *A few lines in "A Parcel of Papers . . . ," the Raleigh story, strike a particular chord, though it takes time to recognize the music; "I think, father, that the difference between us, who are Indians, or half Indians, and people like the Spaniards and the English and the Dutch and the French, people who know how to go where they are going, I think for them the world is a safer place"; are you speaking of the world as a safer place for the colonizer, and saying that when worlds cross and intercon- nect, something happens to make one lose while the other gains?*

VSN: There's an internal irony about that as well. It's essentially true: the world's safer for those who know where they are going, but the man who says that is the aboriginal Indian. He's turned out to be safer than all the people he served. The world will be safer for those who come after from Europe, but it wasn't safer for Raleigh or the Spanish governor; the people the Indian served all died rather badly. So there is a truth, but there's a developing irony in it. One of the themes of that story is also that the enemy becomes the man you love. The chain just goes on and on. You have to break the chain at some stage and say: I can't carry on living like this, it's too painful, let me get away.

AH: *To stay with colonial matters for a moment, you have visited several post-colonial societies and probably have some comments on cultural loss, replacement, borrowing.*

VSN: I don't think that way. History is an interplay of various peoples, and it's gone on forever. I can think of no culture that's been left to itself. It's a very simple view that borrowing just began the other day with the European expansion. Think of all that was brought back by the crusaders from the Middle East. The tiles in churches, the pulpit, all that comes from the mosque. Think of the food we eat and the Arabian coffee and Chinese tea and Mexican chocolate we drink. There's always been this interplay. It continues, but there remain areas of particularity. If you take some literary form without fully understanding its origins and apply it to your own culture, it wouldn't necessarily work. You can't apply George Eliot country society to Burma, or India, for example, but people do try. It's one of the many falsities of the literary novel today. I can't help feeling that the form has done its work.

V. S. Naipaul Talks to Alastair Niven

Alastair Niven / 1995

From *Wasafiri* 21 (Spring 1995), 5–6. Reprinted by permission of *Wasafiri*.

On 15 March 1993 V. S. Naipaul was awarded the first David Cohen British Literature Prize. This Prize, administered by the Arts Council of Great Britain (now the Arts Council of England) seeks to be the supreme accolade for a living British writer and is awarded for a life time's work. Its monetary value is the highest of any literary award in the country, totally £40,000. In an interview specially recorded for the presentation and not previously made public Sir Vidia speaks to Alastair Niven, Director of Literature at the Arts Council, about his writing career. Their conversation has been lightly edited for publication by Dr. Niven.

AN: *Sir Vidia, your cultural background is partly one of great story-telling in India and the Caribbean. Your father's writing is also very important in your work. What drew you particularly to narrative as the way you wanted to express yourself in life?*

VSN: This question about narrative: we should first of all leave out traditional backgrounds because they played no part. One just went to school and led that kind of life rather than being part of a more traditional culture. The novel ambition was given to me by my father. He had derived it from his reading and to me that was where the nobility in writing lay. When I developed problems with moving on, having exhausted the early impulses, I discovered that there was a whole world to write about in other ways. The novel assisted people in the nineteenth century to get at certain aspects of truth that earlier forms like narrative poems and essays couldn't get at, and the novel began to do things that hadn't been done before. That is part of the excitement and the validity of the great nineteenth century work. I also began to feel that those of us who had come after were simply borrowing the form and pouring our own experiences into it. This meant that we were really writing other people's books and falsifying experience, because experience has to find its own form. So a lot of my creative life after the early impulses has been to find the correct form for expressing what I feel and what my experience has been of the many mixed worlds in which I have lived.

AN: *In* The Enigma of Arrival (1987) *you seem to be merging fiction with a kind of documentation. Is that how you saw it, that it was a hybrid form you were creating?*

VSN: No, actually it was very simple the way one thought about that. When I began to write *The Enigma of Arrival* and found myself writing about the English countryside I felt that there had been so much said about it in the English language that this kind of writing immediately set up associations which I had to undo. I had to identify my narrator, my seeing eye, my feeling person. I didn't want to invent a character and give him a bogus adventure to set him there. I thought I should make the writer be myself—let that be true and within that set the fictional composite picture because you can't use real people to hang philosophical ideas about flux and change. That's where creation comes in. So there were the two aspects. To me I didn't do it out of any sense of being experimental. It just seemed natural.

AN: *But you have in fact created a new form. Sir Vidia, you have moved in and out of fiction over the years. Graham Greene tended to describe one set of works, his travel writings, as entertainments, differentiated from his fiction, which he regarded as his serious work. In your case I don't think you make any distinction between the fictional writing and the travel and documentary writing; they are of equal status.*

VSN: Yes, both the fiction writing and the travel writings, or books of enquiry conducted in other countries, are aspects of one's looking at the world one has lived in. They are both equally important. The other thing to remember about the fictional form is that it would have been impossible for me to be a writer and to stick to the same form for forty years. Consider how Dickens developed between 1836 and 1870, and Balzac beginning one kind of romantic drama and ending with his realistic description of France. Twenty or thirty years is a very long time and one has to express the movement of one's soul and of the world.

AN: *You seem to have a great sense of movement in your writing. It's not writing that ever stands still to contemplate, but you look at a world that is constantly in a state of mobility and flux. Is that correct?*

VSN: The world has changed and I am aware more and more that I have lived in this last half of the century when one has been adult and active through a period of the most prodigious change. I am very glad I had the courage to follow difficult instincts about the truth and was therefore able to capture something of the changes in the world, the changes in empire, the changes in the colonised, the changes in countries like India, which from being colonised have developed some new sense of the idea of renewal. These things seem to me immensely important.

AN: *And yet at the end of* In A Free State (1971) *you seem to suggest that we are all engaged in a cycle where things come back to the point at which they had begun, and they go on repeating themselves.*

VSN: At the end of *In A Free State* I remember the writer saying that that was perhaps the purest time when everybody lived in their own little isolated world. I think that what was contained in that observation was the knowledge that such a world probably never existed. The world has always been in a state of movement and flux. I can think of no culture that is entirely of itself, self-generated. Africa has had movements all the time from Roman times; India—people crossed and re-crossed: there is no one thing which is India; Europe: who can carry in his head all the movements of people in Europe? So the world *has* been in movement.

AN: *You began your career by writing satirical and very humorous novels. Your work seems to have become more truly serious over the years, but some people would argue that a sense of comedy and the ebullience of life has disappeared from it.*

VSN: I know that people talk about early comedy and later seriousness. I think that there is a good deal of comedy right through the work, a good deal of humour. It is contained in the actual tone of the writing, which probably comes over best during one's reading of it. I write for the voice. I read aloud at the end of the day what I have written to someone who judges and helps me in that way, help for my reading. The other point is that the early comedy was really hysteria, the hysteria of someone who was worried about his place as a writer and his place in the world. When one is really stressed one makes a lot of jokes. You can make jokes all the time. That's not healthy. The profounder comedy comes from greater security.

AN: And you feel you have achieved that, presumably?

VSN: Yes, I feel I have become more serene because of the work and because of the way I have solved problems in my own mind. It was quite late—I was in my mid 40s—when I felt secure in my writing ability. By that stage I knew I could do certain things. Until then I could really be desperately worried about going on.

AN: *It's that question of 'going on' which has fascinated me about your work over the last twenty years. I wondered what on earth you could do next because each work seemed to be a kind of summing up.* The Enigma of Arrival *especially left me with a sense that it was such a completely achieved work. I really could not see where you went next. The novel seemed to be a form from which you were moving away and yet you presumably would not want just to return to more travel observation. I am trying to imagine the form you might be moving towards now.*

VSN: One must write every book as though it is the final work, the summing up. I can't do things again once I've done them as well as I can do them. For example, having done the last Indian travel book I don't feel that I can go and do it for somewhere else. I've done it. I have taken myself through various stages to writing that kind of book. So it's time to do something else. There are always more things to do. I have a restless mind. It is my age, my health and my vitality that are now getting in the way and making me slow up a little. The world is full of excitement for me. Reality is always changing. It changes constantly and the writer has to find new ways of capturing the reality.

AN: *This is the British Literature Prize and it is in recognition of a British writer. Are you surprised to win it and do you feel that the Britishness of your work is something you have been developing over the years?*

VSN: I haven't thought of being British in that way. I have always been very grateful to the country for allowing me to develop my talent here with absolute freedom. I have never done a single thing which I have not wanted to do. I could not have conducted this career in other countries in Europe for the language reasons and for political reasons. I couldn't have done this in China, Japan or India. I could really have done it only here. I could not even have done it in the United States because the American interest in my subjects and my attitudes occurred very very late. You would not believe this now. No one is more anxious to embrace the oppressed of the world. You would not believe that this has developed in the last ten or fifteen years. It wasn't there before.

The changes have been immense. If you consider small places like the islands of the Caribbean, if you consider their history in the last two hundred years, what they've moved from and where they are, you see they have begun again to undo themselves. That's an immense cyclical thing almost. In *The Mimic Men*, a very early book, one's already seeing the seeds of decay in that situation. When one began to write one simply recorded. One didn't question. Then because I was writing from a certain physical distance and time I began to question and see in a different way from the way I had seen in my earlier books.

The Last Lion

Ahmed Rashid / 1995

From *Far Eastern Economic Review*, 30 (November 1995), 49–50. Reprinted by permission of Ahmed Rashid.

How would you classify the type books you are writing now? Non-fiction? Travel?

There is no need to classify them. They are part of my continuing looking at the world in which I live. This idea of categories is slightly bogus. It assumes that there is only one kind of writing that matters, the so-called creative writing which usually means the novel. I think it is a hangover from the 19th century. I think creative writing can be about art history, biography, history. Every kind of writing can be creative.

My books have been called travel writing, but that can be misleading because in the old days travel writing was essentially done by men describing the routes they were taking . . . What I do is quite different. I travel on a theme. I travel not to write about myself but to look at the world. I travel to make an enquiry. I am not a journalist. I am taking all the gifts of sympathy, observation and curiosity I have developed as a writer. I should also add to that list the gift of narrative. The books I write now, these enquiries are really constructed narratives. There is the narrative of the journey within which there are many little narratives that are part of the larger pattern.

Do you think you will ever go back to writing a pure novel or imaginative fiction again?

I do write imaginative work, but I must say that I hate the word 'novel.' I can no longer understand why it is important to write or read invented stories. I myself don't need that stimulation. I don't need those extravaganzas. There is so much reading, so much understanding of the world that I still have to do. We are living at an extraordinary moment when so much knowledge is available to us that was not available 100 years ago. We can read books about Indian art, Indian history, Southeast Asian cultural history, Chinese art, that were simply not available 100 years ago. I don't see reading as an act of drugging oneself with a narrative. I don't need that. This other kind of reading is immensely exciting for me and there is so much of it to do. I no longer have time for these new works of commercial fiction that are being produced.

There was a time when fiction provided the discoveries of the sort I have been describing earlier. Discoveries about the nature of society, about states, so those works of fiction had a validity over and above the narrative element. I feel that those most important works of fiction were done in the 19th century, remarkably now between 1830–1895. I feel that all that has followed since have been versions of those works. What Balzac was doing was creating and discovering modern France and that remains an immense original achievement, a primary achievement. Flaubert also did the same for France in *Madame Bovary*. It was not just a story about a lady who lost her way through her fantasies. It was a story about France. It was a creation of a whole immense culture. All important works are primary works. Those which are not like those which have gone before. The only good books are primary books.

It is very easy for people now to feel that Asian writing is immensely vital in a way that English writing is not. This is actually not a correct way of looking at it. The vitality comes from the fact that the form is borrowed and this new material is poured into it. When enough of that new material has been poured into this particular borrowed form, the vitality will also appear to go and we will be left with the same question such as who are the new writers in Asia. If you read a Russian writer like Turgenev, his *Hunter's Sketches*, you will think I can do this about the Punjab, the landlords in the Punjab. But you are really not writing your own book. You are writing Turgenev's book all over again. Because content and form are always inseparable. What happens when you pour your content into this borrowed form you ever so slightly distort the material. Different cultures have different ways of feeling, seeing, different visions, ideas of human achievement and behaviour. If you try to write like Hemingway and you are writing about India it will not match.

I also think that forms are dynamic. Before the novel in Europe there was the essay, the narrative poem, theatre, the epic poem, these were all considered the principle forms at various times. There is no need for us to consider the novel now as the principal form. I do not know how we can judge a derivative form. People say you look for the story, the characters, the style and you weigh it up. But with primary work you never have to do that, you know it is primary. The fact that people can teach novels and fiction writing in the universities confirms what I am saying. If you can teach people the form in which they can pour their material, about being in Ceylon or Japan, it means that is all you are looking for then. You are not looking for the sensibility of the writer. You are judging the material he has poured into the straitjacket of this borrowed form. I read Southeast Asian novels recently which appeared to have nothing to do with Burma, but everything to do with America and the universities there. Often when I am reading criticism from Asia or Africa, I feel I am reading criticism from the U.S.A.

How is fiction standing up to TV, the computer and the culture of the dish antenna? Is anyone going to be reading fiction in 20 years' time?
I am delighted by all these stories. It will have an extraordinary effect on imaginative writing. People soon feel when they get a book that they want a different experience than what they can get from the visual media. The book will have to speak more directly to their imaginations and their intelligence and sensibilities. It can do nothing but good. It will elevate the idea of writing.

What are you working on now?
I am making a few Islamic excursions.

What other books are seething in your mind?
I would rather not tell you because nothing might happen. I am superstitious. When I was young I never numbered my pages for fear that it was too arrogant and that I would not come to the end. Another thing that I did was that I never wrote my own name on the finished book that I sent to the publisher. These are little acts of magic. I have lost all this magic now and I am very shameless and I put in my name and number the pages.

How have you adapted to the computer age? Do you still write long hand or can you turn out thousands of words a day on a laptop?
I have never turned out thousands of words. I do it by hand and when I am going very well I do about 400 words in a good day and I have perhaps three good days a week. I write very slowly and by hand and then transfer it to the screen. I transfer half a page to the screen and then I can print it out and play with it.

Your style is uncontrived and easy to read. What is the process of arriving at such a style?
I am not pleased when people tell me I have a nice style. It suggests that style is something applied. It is not. Style in itself has no value. I just try to write as clearly as I can to let those thoughts appear on the page. I don't want the style to stand out, I don't want the words to get in the way. I wish to create something the reader does not notice and which he reads very quickly. It took a lot of work to do it. In the beginning I had to forget everything I had written by the age of 22. I abandoned every-

Index